WaS ThiS in tHE PLAn?

Stephanie Nimmo

Hashtag PRESS

This edition published in Great Britain by Hashtag Press 2017

A CIP catalogue for this book is available from the British Library.

ISBN 978-0-9957806-2-0

Typeset in Garamond Classic 11.25/14 by Blaze Typesetting

Printed in Great Britain by Clays Ltd, St Ives plc

HASHTAG PRESS BOOKS
Hashtag Press Ltd
Kent, England, United Kingdom
Email: info@hashtagpress.co.uk
Website: www.hashtagpress.co.uk
Twitter: @hashtag_press

For Andy

Acknowledgements
My love and thanks

To our parents and our Scottish and Welsh families. To our friends, all over the world, who have walked our path with us for many years.

To my friends who I call on in a crisis, you know who you are. You are my avengers; you women sustain me and without you I don't know how I would cope.

To the class of '86—it took me a long time to realise that our time together gave me the resilience to be the person I am today.

To the Doctors, Nurses, Carers, Therapists, Administrators and Support Staff we have met on the way—thank you for making a difference.

To the Social Care teams—thank you for fighting my corner.

To the Educators, the SenCos, the counsellors and therapists—thank you for never giving up.

To everyone at Shooting Star Chase—thank you for walking our path with us.

To all the other warrior mothers and fathers and carers out there—I hope I have helped shine a light on our world.

To the people who have been part of our story: Janet Swain, Simon Bell, Marion Germain, Alison Bourne, John Nimmo, Sam Carlisle, Sarah Collins, Niki & Steve Brown, Lynne & Phil Wilkins, Thijs & AnneMarie, Astrid & Edwin, Gary Elden and everyone at Sthree past and present, Keith Southern, Lee Grantham, Alex MacLeod, Scott Ransome, Jon & Suzanne, Jon & Fiona, Chris & Sue, Peter Serafinowitz, Benedict Wong, Helen Linehan, Gaby Skolnek and Jo Whiley.

For helping me shape this story into something people

might actually want to read; Helen & Abiola at Hashtag, Jemima Hunt and Sam Carlisle.

Most of all I want to thank my incredible family:
Andy, Theo, Xanthe, Jules and Daisy.
I am me because of you.
Thank you.

"It's times like these you learn to live again
It's times like these you give and give again
It's times like these you learn to love again
It's times like these time and time again"
- Foo Fighters -

FOREWORD

By Jo Whiley, Radio DJ and Television Presenter

No one has taught me more to relish life than Steph. I first heard from her via a tweet she'd sent me. I get many tweets so I've no idea why I replied to her. She'd written to me asking if I could help her fulfil her husband Andy's bucket list. He wanted to see the Foo Fighters at potentially his final Glastonbury and if possible meet the band who he'd long-time worshipped from afar.

I began to check that Steph's message was bona fide and my research lead me to her blog and the title of this book—*'Was This in the Plan?'*. I remember feeling a connection instantly. Steph and Andy had four children whom they plainly adored. They were formidable characters with a robust sense of humour, they were HUGE music fans and they lived life to the full. But their life was complicated. And then some.

Daisy had extremely complex needs and a life limiting condition. Andy had been diagnosed with terminal cancer and Steph had no choice but to juggle caring for both of them with being Mum to Xanthe, Theo and Jules. The least I could do was engineer a meeting with a rock band. Thankfully Andy got to meet Dave Grohl who was as epic as Andy wanted him to be and didn't let him down. Phew! From that point on our lives became entwined.

First of all we tweeted, then we texted, and finally we met up and ate cake in a fancy London department store where we got on brilliantly, as I knew we would. I have a sister with learning difficulties so I knew something of Daisy's world. Both Daisy and my sister Frances would occasionally surprise strangers with a hefty thump for no apparent reason #awkward.

My mum has always been a warrior and I recognised this in Steph. A wife, mother and campaigner who will stop at nothing to care for the people she loves and to make every day count. By sharing her family's story, Steph speaks to others who are dealing with their own challenges and personal tragedies. Showing us that no matter what life throws at you, there is an inner strength within us all and that as painful as it can be at times, life is there to be lived to the full.

What has happened to Steph is mind-bogglingly heart-breaking or as Steph puts it succinctly, *"it's just monumentally shit."* It's been a privilege to get to know the Nimmo family. They've changed my perspective of life and death. I now have a much greater appreciation and understanding of both. Steph has spoken of the ripples that Daisy left behind, how she touched so many people's lives and this is undeniably true. But it's also true of Steph and she should know that.

She's a crazy, crusading, running, swimming, music-loving, gin-swigging lady. What's not to love and admire?

PROLOGUE

"There's a problem with this machine. I'm just going to get someone."

We were at the hospital for our early dating scan for Nimmo Baby Number Four. I'd not been able to shake off the feeling of wanting one more, to round off the family, to even out the numbers. Four children would complete us; we had always said we wanted a big family, after all, my husband, Andy, didn't need much persuading. If we had really thought things through, we would have stopped at two—but despite the chaos and the ever-increasing laundry mountain, we loved having children and didn't want it to stop, at least not yet.

When Andy and I first discussed starting a family we thought it would take twelve months or more to conceive and so we decided to have a year of fun, travelling and going to exotic places while we tried. But then I fell pregnant within the month, which put our plans to travel to India and Sri Lanka on hold. Instead, we had an extended trip along the north and west French coasts, taking in the D-Day landing beaches in Normandy, eating crêpes in Brittany, photographing the sunflower fields in the Vendée and visiting the cognac factories in Charente-Maritime.

It was on a return holiday with the children in Normandy a few years later that I found out I was pregnant again. Our family of five was to become six. By now we thought we had the whole pregnancy and birth thing down to a fine art.

I was planning another home water birth and wanted to have as little to do with this hospital and medical stuff as possible. We only needed to go there for the scans and antenatal clinics and that suited me.

The doctor returned, accompanied by a nurse. What we didn't know then was that this was a very special nurse. This was the nurse only a few people met, the nurse who came to speak to you when an anomaly was detected on the ultrasound scan.

"We think there is a problem with the baby," the doctor said cautiously, clearly knowing he was about to deliver a huge bombshell. "Our calculations show that statistically it is at high risk of having Down's syndrome."

"How high?" I responded. "What are the stats?"

We were used to our risk factors being in the thousands, but maybe because we were older this time we were looking at one in several hundred? That's okay, that's still good odds...

"One in four."

Our baby had a one-in-four risk of having Down's syndrome. So there was still a seventy-five percent chance it didn't have Down's, wasn't there?

We were numb. All I could think was, what had we done? Why had we been so greedy as to want another baby when we already had three perfect children at home, waiting for us?

We hugged and cried and then we went home with an appointment to return in the next few days for chorionic villus sampling (CVS), an invasive antenatal test where a sample of amniotic fluid would be taken for analysis to establish whether or not our baby had Down's.

I could not get the thought out of my head: what if our baby *was* disabled? Had we ruined our children's lives forever? I looked around at my perfect life, my perfect marriage, my perfect children. What if our much-wanted son or daughter did test positive for Down's? How the hell would we cope with a disabled child? Would we keep it?

"No way," I thought. *"This wasn't in the plan!"*

CHAPTER ONE

"I don't like Jon's friend much, he's really full of himself and tells crap jokes."

Ali and I were in the ladies' toilet of the Three Compasses Pub in Canterbury, Kent. It was Jon's birthday, 5th October 1988. He was an army officer stationed in the nearby barracks and had been dating our friend, Bee, for the past few months. His friends had come along for the evening to help him celebrate. Little did I know that I had just met the love of my life.

Andy was holding court at the table, doing his best to impress the assembled group of army officers and university students. He was regaling everyone with stories of life on the building site where he was working. I noticed his hair had a peppering of grey, he had sharp blue eyes and he was clearly enjoying playing to his captive audience as he shared his slightly risqué anecdotes.

He seemed to be very knowledgeable about most things and was clearly highly intelligent, and I wondered why he wasn't at university or in the army like the rest of us around the table. We started chatting. He was out to impress and it was not long before our conversation turned to music.

Having travelled a lot, he had wide and varied musical tastes. We scanned the juke box, discussing the merits of different tracks, trying to catch each other out on our knowledge of obscure bands.

Away from the rest of the group, Andy seemed a bit less cocky, more sensitive. He explained that his job was temporary, to make money in order to take advantage of the property development boom that was sweeping South East England at that time.

"As soon as I've saved up a deposit for a flat, I'm done," he said.

We talked a lot that evening, not just about music, but also about current affairs, travelling, politics and our mutual dislike of the Thatcher government and all it stood for. By the end of the evening I had really warmed to him and hoped that we would see each other again.

* * *

I was brought up in the Victorian seaside town of Penarth in South Wales, the eldest of two girls. It was a halcyon upbringing spent playing on beaches, drinking frothy coffees in Rabaiotti's café, late-night swimming with the boys in Cosmeston Lakes, Friday night underage drinking at the Railway Pub, skipping school to go to the Radio One Roadshow on Barry Island. I spent the summers cycling around the lanes of the Vale of Glamorgan, shopping in nearby Cardiff or splashing in the waves at Southerndown Beach.

I was a conscientious student and my parents and teachers encouraged me to apply for a scholarship at a prestigious international sixth form college in South Wales. The United

World College of the Atlantic gave me a way of escaping my hometown and expanding my horizons. In those days, our local council funded three scholarships.

The interview process was gruelling. Having filled in an exhaustive application form, we were led through a day of activities alongside the other applicants where our every move was observed and documented before being grilled in a panel interview. I talked about my membership of the Campaign for Nuclear Disarmament (CND) and my involvement with our local anti-apartheid group, how I had persuaded my parents to stop buying South African goods in protest. I spoke of my desire to travel and see the world; how I wanted to make a difference and how the scholarship would be a springboard to do both.

To my astonishment, when the letter finally came I was offered a full scholarship. In September 1986, three months after my sixteenth birthday, my mum drove me through the gates of Atlantic College to join a sea of young people, all speaking different languages, all looking equally as nervous as me.

I lay in bed that night in my dorm, wondering what I had done. Had I made the right decision to come here? There was certainly no going back now.

My first encounter with the college had been on a family open day many years earlier when the castle and its extensive grounds had been opened to the public. I'd swum in the outdoor pool, gazing up at the imposing St Donat's Castle perched high up overlooking the sea, surrounded by ornate rose gardens. It was like a picture postcard.

Now here I was, aged sixteen, catapulted from small town life to a castle previously owned by American newspaper magnate William Randolph Hearst, living with young people from all over the world. I no longer had the comfort and security of my local school, nor my own room, I was now sharing a dorm with two girls I had never met before and a bathroom with twenty others. While most of the students spoke different languages and were from all four corners of the world, it was as much of a culture shock for me, a local girl, as it was for them.

Atlantic College was founded by the German educationalist Kurt Hahn. He wanted to bring together young minds from all over the globe to live and study together in the spirit of what he called *'international understanding'*.

He also founded the Outward Bound organisation and there was a big focus on outdoor pursuits and physical activity at the school as a result. Everyone had to be able to swim and a daily dose of fresh air could not be avoided as we made our way around the blustery grounds going to our lessons.

We studied for the International Baccalaureate Diploma, still relatively new in the UK at the time. I majored in German, Biology and English with Maths, Marine Science and Economics as subsidiary subjects. There was also a compulsory course called Theory of Knowledge and an extended research essay. It was a huge academic workload for someone who only a few months before had been taking O levels at the local comprehensive school.

We were required to further expand our minds by becoming involved in community service projects and by learning a variety of new skills. I taught canoeing to young people who had been excluded from school and I learned to sail in the choppy waters of the Bristol Channel. In March 1985, I had the chance to visit Soviet Russia as part of a school delegation, attending a reception in the Kremlin and finding myself in Moscow when the incumbent Russian President, Konstantin Chernenko, died suddenly.

It was at Atlantic College that I learned resilience. Not only did living away from home with young people from all over the world mean that I had to grow up quickly, but we were fairly isolated in a castle perched on a cliff overlooking the Bristol Channel. It was also inevitable that some of our time was spent scaling those cliffs, often ending up submerged in icy sea water.

It took me many years to realise that the *'great'* things spoken of by my school's founder didn't have to be *big* things. For a long time after I left Atlantic College I worried that I had failed in some way, that I was not a great politician or humanitarian, a doctor or a teacher. So many of my contemporaries had gone on to do great things: lead charity projects, enter politics, give back to their communities. Yet, in retrospect, the school's ethos set me up for life; it would come to serve me well in ways I could not then imagine. It also gave me an incredible network of close friends all over the world.

Leaving school is never easy, and for us, cocooned in our castle by the sea with our idealism and plans to change the world, re-entry into society came as a shock. In September 1986–the year that journalist John McCarthy was kidnapped in Beirut, Mrs Thatcher was *still* our Prime Minister and Nelson Mandela was *still* a prisoner on Robben Island–I landed at the University of Kent to study for a degree in social anthropology.

* * *

'The environmental impact of the Kwakiutl Potlatch Ceremony' was the title of my dissertation. I was in my second year, having spent the previous year in British Columbia gathering research information for my dissertation, as well as learning

to ski, catching up with school friends and hitchhiking in the Rocky Mountains. I was twenty, young, free, single and ready to change the world. In between boycotting South African oranges and campaigning for CND, I attended lectures and tutorials on subjects as diverse as Systems of Ritual and Belief, The Sociology of Deviance and Health, and Wellness and Society. Some of my friends, busy studying law and accountancy, thought anthropology was a Mickey Mouse degree, but they couldn't have been more wrong.

I was learning to view the world from the perspective of an outsider. I loved the debate, the analysis and reflection, again all useful tools for later life when I would need to remain objective, formulating coherent arguments and working out the best scenario to fit our many challenges. My anthropology studies have always helped me stand in someone else's shoes and see the world from *their* eyes.

I relished my time at university; the parties, friendships, the new-found knowledge. I felt empowered. I was going to take on the world and I was certainly not ready to settle down. '*Girls Just Wanna Have Fun*' sang Cyndi Lauper, and I had plans.

CHAPTER TWO

"Fancy a drink in the Compasses?"

It was a job in Kent that led Andy to the Three Compasses pub for Jon's birthday. His work was only a few miles away so it was easy to meet up in Canterbury where Jon was based with his army regiment. It's funny how the fates conspired for us to meet. I had taken a year out after my first year at university and spent my time travelling and gathering research, ready to go back for the second year. Had I *not* taken that year out, it's unlikely I would have met Ali, who had returned to Canterbury after a gap year in Germany. On that day we had both tired of studying.

"Fancy a drink in the Compasses?" she asked. "This essay can wait until Sunday night."

I didn't take much persuading and grabbed my coat.

Andy was born in Kilmarnock, Scotland, the youngest of two. By the time he was nine, his family had upped sticks and moved to the new town of Basingstoke in Hampshire, where there were better employment opportunities for his parents. His cousins lived a few doors away and together they roamed the local countryside. Andy was not academic; the education system was no match for his free spirit. I still have a copy of his primary school report in which his teacher comments: '*He enjoys entertaining the rest of the class and the only activity he excels in is reading, which he would happily do all day*'.

His first love was drama. He won a scholarship to attend summer school at the National Youth Theatre (along with an equally young and enthusiastic Colin Firth) and he always said that his time spent at the NYT was the best of his life. Here was a new world that was his for the taking.

Andy was six years older than me, and while I'd been in junior school he was part of the local punk scene, making weekly journeys to London to go to gigs. He was often armed with a camera, capturing the spirit of the 1970s on film. Come the 1980s, and while I was working hard at Atlantic College, he was a holiday rep at Club 18-30 in Greece, perfecting his chat-up lines and dance routines.

He walked out of school weeks before he was due to sit his A levels, bored and uninspired by academic study. Andy had been told by his teachers he was spending too much time in the drama studio rather than revising. He phoned his mother from a call box in Dover to say that he was going travelling and he would see her soon.

He hitched across Europe, travelling down the Portuguese coast, then heading north to Holland, where he found work on an organic farm. A drunken (and probably very stoned) night in Amsterdam led to a tattoo of a butterfly on his bottom. It was only when he was in his thirties that his mother found out about that tattoo; I had let it slip in conversation.

Back in the UK, Andy resolved to become part of the property boom. Office blocks were springing up all over

London and the South East. Andy blagged his way onto a building site and became a curtain wall fixer and glazier (years later we would drive past buildings in London and he would point out windows he had fitted in office blocks).

Despite the inauspicious start in the Three Compasses, we fell for each other in a big way.

"Where exactly is Basingstoke?" I asked him as I checked the map. He, in turn, had never been to Wales.

I soon saw beyond the crap jokes and cocky attitude. I loved Bowie and Dylan, he had seen the Clash seven times. We both loved the Beatles. We discussed politics, religion and current affairs. Conversations were always heated and we both had strong views on everything. We loved to cook, we enjoyed singing along to the radio, we got drunk together. We fell in love and, had Facebook existed, we would have changed our statuses on 20th April 1989 to '*in a relationship*'.

Our first flat was just outside Canterbury's city walls, on the top floor of an ancient, draughty building. Friends came to stay, our families visited. We didn't have much money, this was always a theme in our lives, but we had conversation, wine, John Peel's late night sessions on BBC Radio 1 and an endless supply of videos from the shop opposite.

Andy loved films. He introduced me to his all-time favourite film, '*Apocalypse Now*', and to Harrison Ford in '*Blade Runner*'.

"OK, let's redress the balance," I would respond. "Time for a John Hughes film. Have you ever seen 'The Breakfast Club'?"

We would quote our favourite lines from '*Withnail and I*'. We laughed a lot. We made plans. We were going to be together forever.

I was in my last year at university, writing up my dissertation, studying for my finals. Andy was still working on building sites to support us, but he was also auditioning for drama schools. On 11th February 1990, I put aside my revision and we both watched the live coverage of Nelson Mandela walking free from prison. We had both campaigned against apartheid and now a new era had begun.

That summer I finished my exams and we moved to London. Andy had won a scholarship to attend the post-graduate drama course at the Academy of Live and Recorded Arts in Wandsworth, as a mature student. I had been offered a graduate traineeship in marketing with a new upcoming telecoms company, Mercury Communications. We still partied hard. Andy worked part-time in Sainsbury's to supplement our income and I commuted to the Docklands every day, passing building sites where only a year previously Andy had been working.

We were now living in Raynes Park in South West London, sharing a flat with Ali. She had graduated the year before me, moving up to London ahead of us, and was working in media sales. London was a graduate's paradise. It did not matter that I had a Mickey Mouse degree in anthropology; employers wanted my skills.

Andy went to drama school every day, living his dream, relishing every moment of it, inhabiting new characters, new worlds. This was his chance to perform alongside students from all over the world and spend time in the drama studio on a full-time basis at long last. He was thrilled on graduating to land his first paid job, a pantomime at the Theatre Royal in Hull. The production of 'Dick Whittington' starred Bernie Nolan and the comedians Cannon and Ball. Andy was the assistant stage manager as well as playing an assortment of minor roles.

"In years to come my interpretation of 'Man in Shop' and 'The Grand Vizier' will be held up as some of the finest moments in British theatre!" laughed Andy.

That Christmas was spent at a student hostel in Hull, smuggling in alcohol and breaking the rules by sharing a room despite being unmarried.

Our friends were getting married. It was just assumed that we would too. We both knew we wanted children and I could not imagine spending the rest of my life with anyone else: he had become my best friend as well as my lover.

"So, shall we get married then?" he asked, somewhat unromantically, as he got down on one knee and presented me with a beautiful emerald engagement ring during a holiday that summer in the South of France.

Andy was by then a professional Equity card-carrying actor. He was working regularly, not the glamorous gigs of the A-listers perhaps, but still a *working* actor. I, meanwhile, still worked at Mercury Communications while also studying in the evening for my professional marketing qualifications.

We scraped together enough cash to buy a very run-down flat in Earlsfield, an upcoming area of Wandsworth in South West London. To say the flat needed modernisation was an understatement. It needed everything doing to it. It still had the original outside loo, but it didn't matter—we had our own place, and it had a garden! In typical Andy and Steph style we put our house renovation plans on hold and decided to plan our wedding. If anything it was just another excuse for a party, and far more interesting than discussing party wall agreements.

We were married on 12th September 1992, in Dinas Powys, South Wales. Andy wore his kilt, someone sang a solo in Welsh and family and friends travelled from all over to be with us and share our special day. During the evening party there was a spontaneous karaoke session.

"Fly me to the moon and let me play among the stars, let me see what spring is like on Jupiter and Mars..." Andy sang to me, doing his cheesiest Sinatra impression.

His brother, John, an accomplished boogie-woogie pianist, played piano and there was even a bit of Scottish dancing.

Mrs Stephanie Nimmo.

I loved being married to Andy. I loved promising to be with him 'til death do us part. Take away the dress, the flowers and the party and it was all about Andy and me, vowing to stick together, whatever life threw at us.

CHAPTER THREE

"Dad, I'm thinking of training for the Cardiff Marathon."

Dad had always been a runner. As a young man he had struggled academically but excelled at sports: rugby, swimming, athletics. Throughout my childhood he would take off on Sunday mornings to train and I would loyally watch his races, waiting on the start line as the runners stood around keeping warm by wearing black bin liners. There were no GPS watches or specialist diets, just enthusiasm and a shared camaraderie. Dad introduced me to running and in 1981 we ran the inaugural Cardiff Marathon together. At thirteen, I was one of the youngest runners and one of very few women participating. I think it was one of his proudest moments.

Dad left his legacy to the running community in Wales in the form of the *Welsh Castles Relay*, a team relay race, which runs overnight from North to South Wales, castle to castle. These days it's a landmark race on the running calendar with corporate sponsors, a ballot for club entries and the involvement of many volunteers and organisers. When Dad put forward the idea at his running club AGM for a relay to mark the Welsh

Year of the Castle in 1982 he would never know how big it would become. That summer our family holiday was spent travelling in our ancient Morris Minor from South Wales to North Wales working out the Castles Relay route with the help of the car's milometer.

Although Cardiff had been my first marathon, my social life and studies got in the way of my running for a while. Years later we decided it was time for another father-daughter marathon adventure and we entered the London Marathon.

We put in our training over the winter, Dad in Wales, me in London and in 1996, on a sunny spring day, we found ourselves on the start line in Greenwich Park. This time I beat Dad, although to be fair neither of us were very speedy runners; we just relied on grit and determination to get around the course.

By now I had even managed to encourage Andy to do a little bit of running. A couple of months after the London Marathon we ran the Basingstoke Half Marathon together. This time my legs felt like lead and I couldn't understand why. I had put in more hours training than Andy but he was beating me?

I soon had my answer.

On my twenty-eighth birthday, in June 1996 I found out I was pregnant with a much wanted first child. After seven years together we were going to become parents and start a new chapter of our lives.

I'd progressed through the ranks at Mercury Communications, working long hours as marketing manager on the team bidding to secure the contract to build and run the Police National Network (PNN). The PNN would connect the fifty-three police forces throughout the UK; previously each was operating independently with minimal co-ordinated sharing of data. We won the bid and I was there when Home Secretary Michael Howard signed the contract.

Andy was a jobbing actor. He had a couple of tours and a repertory season under his belt, along with some TV work, voiceovers and adverts. He had worked as an actor guide for a couple of seasons at the Museum of the Moving Image on the South Bank in London, indulging his love for film with his talent for acting. He auditioned for the first ever officially-licensed stage production of Star Trek and was offered the role of Scotty. It was a big break in acting terms.

Life was good for Mr and Mrs Nimmo. It got even better when Theodore Thomas Nimmo came into our lives on 8th February 1997. Surprising us by arriving a week early, he weighed a healthy six pounds eleven ounces. As if to make his mark on the world, Theo was born with his hand on his head necessitating a ventouse delivery after nearly two days of labouring on my part. None of the pain of the previous few days (or even the pregnancy) mattered once I held him in my arms.

"We really are a family now," I said to Andy.

"Blimey, this is all so grown up and real, isn't it?" he replied.

Back at home, the reality of parenthood hit us. We were now responsible for this little person! There was no instruction manual and Theo depended on us twenty-four/seven. We were very much making it up as we went along.

Andy had another contract for a season at the Museum of the Moving Image at the time and was able to be pretty flexible about being at home. He was a really hands-on dad, changing nappies, winding Theo after his feeds. Theo was very windy, in fact he was very colicky.

Did babies really cry all the time like that? Was it me? I changed my diet in case my breast milk affected him, we tried colic drops and cranial osteopathy, but he did not sleep much and was very unsettled. Maybe it was because he was our first? We were trying to be relaxed and not stress too much, but life with new-born Theo was hard work and at times I found myself almost hallucinating with tiredness.

On 1st May 1997 Labour swept into power with a landslide victory. As new parents, we were filled with hope. Here was a new government that understood us, that really represented us. Andy stayed up most of the night watching the coverage and the next day went to work on the South Bank where the victory parties continued. There was an extraordinary sense of optimism in the air.

With Theo's arrival, we realised we had outgrown our flat, despite its spare bedroom and garden. We started looking for bigger properties and acknowledged that we would have to compromise and move to an outer London borough. One sunny weekend we walked into the house that was to become our home. It was bright and spacious and had (for London) a big garden. We put an offer in straight away and by June we had moved in.

Andy had started to branch out into teaching presentation skills to business executives. Touring and Equity minimum rates were not conducive to a happy family life and Andy wanted to be with his wife and son. He was a working actor but to really hit the big time he needed to network when all he really wanted to do was be at home with us.

He enjoyed the training work, and working alongside other consultants expanded his own skills. He began to think that this was something he'd like to do on a full-time basis. He was a natural. People warmed to him, he enjoyed the instant feedback of the training room and his experiences of life gave him valuable insights as he worked with his clients. He gained a professional qualification in Neuro-Linguistic Programming and coaching and progressed later to secure his Master's Certification – all this from the man who hated academic life and had walked out of school before sitting his A levels.

My successful track record at Mercury Communications meant that my skills and experience were in demand and I was headhunted to take up a marketing role at Hewlett-Packard.

Andy had a gift for training and coaching and soon this was to eclipse acting and become his primary income source. He had begun travelling with his work and childcare became a juggling act as one or other of us jetted off to an exciting location. He would be in Rio delivering a big training programme, then I would fly off to Tokyo to work on a project for Hewlett-Packard. As a marketing lead in the company's professional services division, I would fly to San Francisco every six weeks. I once flew back from Washington, D.C. to be with the family for the weekend and then returned the following week for the rest of my meetings.

Twenty-five months after Theo arrived, I gave birth to our daughter, Xanthe Flora. Such a different delivery from the first time, Xanthe was just a day past her due date, a completely natural birth. I delivered her in a birth pool at Chelsea and Westminster Hospital and Andy cut the cord. She had a mop of thick black hair that stood up in spikes, so we nicknamed her Posh Spice. Andy was ecstatic. The nurse had to ask him to stop singing along so loudly to our birth mixtape as it was one o'clock in the morning and he was disturbing the other labouring mothers.

We brought Xanthe home to her brother as soon as possible

and I threw myself into the pink loveliness of having a girl. Theo was obsessed with Thomas the Tank Engine and Fireman Sam, so it was going to be wonderful to have an opportunity to redress the balance of males in the house.

Andy wasn't the only one gaining new qualifications and skills. I had also finished my Master's degree in marketing while on maternity leave in order to further my career. I decided to reduce my travelling commitments now that I had two children and took up an account director role at one of the many new media agencies springing up in London at the time. My skills and experience in technology marketing for blue chip firms were in demand and I found myself working on the agency's big accounts, Shell and Barclaycard, as they ventured into the world of e-commerce. It was great to have the buzz of the agency, working late shifts to complete proposals, presenting to clients, working with creatives.

I regret giving away my tickets to a gig in order to finish a pitch, I don't even remember what the pitch was for, but I do remember missing one of the last ever Spice Girls gigs.

CHAPTER FOUR

"Happy New Year! Happy New Millennium!"

It was the turn of the century. I was at the top of my game professionally, riding the dot-com wave, Andy's new career in training and development was taking off, we had a house in the suburbs, a son and a daughter, two cats. Life for the Nimmos was good. The new year was fast approaching and the hot topic was where you would be when the clock struck midnight and we entered a new century. This was closely followed by concerns about the millennium bug and whether the world was going to end.

Who knew?

My extended family converged on Littlehampton, West Sussex, the scene of many happy New Year's Eves spent as guests of my parents' friends when we were growing up. It seemed the natural place for us all to be on this very special new year.

Mum and Dad drove from Wales and my sister and her husband came down from Middlesex. Dad seemed a bit subdued, but I put it down to work; I thought he must have something on his mind, but didn't ask. Dad was normally the life and soul of the party, the gentle giant who rarely drank but told a great story, enjoyed the company of friends and most of all spending time with his new grandchildren. Theo called him Dada.

I bought Dad a mobile phone for Christmas. He wasn't particularly technology savvy, preferring the VHF radio he used in his role as a volunteer coastguard. But in the new year, he used his phone to call his doctor. He had seen a poster for the Bobby Moore Cancer Fund in the men's washroom at the headquarters of South Wales Police where he worked. It listed the worrying symptoms he had been experiencing and told no one about: bleeding from the bottom, unexplained weight loss, fatigue.

Dad had just turned sixty-one. His doctor always said he had the heart of a twenty year old, to which Dad's stock response was, "Well, you'd better give it back to him then!"

The doctor didn't think there was anything seriously wrong with Dad, probably just a case of haemorrhoids, but nevertheless sent him for tests, including a colonoscopy.

I was at work on 14th February 2000 when I had a call from Andy. My dad had been diagnosed with advanced colorectal cancer. By the time it was found and my parents had waded through the NHS bureaucracy, it had spread to his liver.

Those were the days before the big shake up in cancer care, when disjointed paths of communication were commonplace. A time before cancer care pathways, designed to improve communication, and a multi-disciplinary team approach were established to save lives and reduce treatment waiting times.

Dad had hoped to benefit from a new technique used to target the tumours in his liver directly with chemotherapy, however the liver surgeon had not felt he was a suitable candidate, yet neglected to inform either my dad or the oncologist. The series of delays was very stressful and the stress was compounded when Dad developed a deep vein thrombosis, further delaying any surgery or chemotherapy.

Eventually Dad had the much-anticipated surgery to remove as much of the primary tumour as possible. We were all relieved; at last he could begin chemotherapy treatment and start focusing on beating this thing.

Even more delays ensued, however, and one day I got so fed up I marched into the nurse manager's office.

"What is going on with my dad?" I demanded. "There doesn't seem to be any plan. People keep coming to see him but he doesn't know what's happening about his treatment."

"Mrs Nimmo," she replied. "You do know your father's cancer is incurable? Once it's in the liver it's time for the palliative care team to be involved."

I felt like I had been punched in the stomach. Palliative care team? This was the first time it had been mentioned.

"Does my dad know this?" I asked.

"Well, I can get the palliative care nurse to come and speak to him," came her response.

I had to return to my dad's bedside to give him the news. The small detail that the teams involved in his care had neglected to mention was that he would *not* be cured of this cancer. Chemotherapy was only going to buy him time.

Dad focused on getting strong for chemo. He played motivational music on the Walkman I bought him (I still can't listen to *Eye of the Tiger* without thinking of my dad). The surgery had debilitated him and there were daily injections to thin his blood and break down the DVT. Chemotherapy was brutal, even for a six-foot three-inch former rugby player who, only a few months previously, was cycling a ten-mile round trip to work each day.

I was in a meeting with a new client who had received millions of pounds from venture capitalists to launch a dot-com start up and wanted our agency to turn their vision into reality, when my phone rang. I excused myself to take the call. It was my mother.

"He's dying, Steph," she said.

Making my apologies, I rushed home. Andy and I bundled the children into the car. We picked up my pregnant sister en route to Wales. Simon, her husband, followed later by train.

My father died on 26th October 2000, with all of us by his side. Until the day he died he believed he could beat his cancer. He was on the main ward of a hospital with the curtains around him, having refused to transfer to a hospice. That, in his eyes, would have meant giving in. He was sixty-one and had not even retired from work.

The night Dad died, his former teammates at Les Croupiers Running Club in Cardiff held a minute's silence in his honour.

Dad's funeral was a bittersweet occasion, a celebration of a life well lived with the sadness of a life cut short. His coffin was carried into the crematorium accompanied by his favourite Tony Bennett track '*The Good Life*' and I delivered the eulogy. Andy conducted the humanist service and when the time came to close the curtains of the crematorium around the coffin, Andy pressed the button and Dad was gone. '*You'll Never Walk Alone*' played through the crematorium speakers, the flag of Penarth's volunteer coastguard service of which he had been a long-standing member, lowered in respect.

We held my father's wake at the same hotel where we had celebrated our wedding eight years previously. The staff still remembered my dad; he had always waved hello as he passed on one of his regular training runs. Dad was a local legend, an unforgettable character, and his loss resonated through our family. It was a turning point for all of us in more ways than we knew.

CHAPTER FIVE

"Andy, I think you need to go and chat to the GP. I'm worried that you are just not your usual happy self these days."

After spending a fortnight in Wales sorting out all the practicalities and arranging Dad's funeral, I came home and immediately returned to work. I had barely had time to process what had just happened.

Dad's cancer and death were a trigger for so many things in our lives. Xanthe was only eighteen months old when he died but Theo was three and a half, so we had to have some tricky conversations with him about death and dying.

Andy and my dad had been very close and his death hit him hard. He felt lethargic and lost his motivation to work. With Andy working freelance, I was now the major wage earner and we had two energetic toddlers who demanded our constant attention.

When Andy found it difficult to get out of bed and out of the house in the morning, I knew he needed help. I asked him to go and talk to our wonderful doctor and I wasn't entirely surprised when he came home to say that he'd been diagnosed with depression.

This was the first real test of our marriage. Within only eight years we had moved to a new house, changed careers, had two children and now faced our first experience of bereavement. But we worked through it and as a couple it made us stronger. With the support of our doctor, Andy started on antidepressants and talking therapy. As it turned out, Andy stayed on the tablets for the rest of his life. He was realistic that the drugs helped give him the window of light he needed to focus and to be able to get on with life. To his credit, he was not ashamed of his depression; it was controlled and, in his case, relatively mild.

In the spring of 2001 we had come to the conclusion that we both needed stability and Andy's freelance training work was failing to provide that, with the unpredictability of it adding to our stress. Andy started work as a training consultant at Sthree, a large and growing recruitment firm. It was here that Andy met some of his closest friends and built a career that would sustain him for the years to come.

Most evenings, after the children had gone to bed, we would open a bottle of wine and collapse on the sofa, surrounded by the chaos of toys, school books and discarded shoes and socks. We loved our children, hearing their stories about their achievements, and heartaches in school, followed by bath time bubbles and cuddling them up in big towels while listening to their plans and dreams.

"My favourite thing in the world is curtsies," Xanthe would say in her high voice, while Theo enthused about the latest Thomas the Tank Engine train he needed for his collection.

It was during one of these evenings that I said to Andy, "What are your thoughts on three?"

"What do you mean?" he said, knowing full well what was coming next.

From our very early days we knew we were never going to stop at two children. We each had one sibling and envied our cousins who came from bigger families.

"Yes, you know, a third?" I continued.

Andy didn't need much persuading. He might complain about the chaos and the mess, but Andy loved being a parent as much as I did. The actor in him relished his adoring, captive audience. There was never a shortage of long, convoluted, funny stories, complete with comedy voices and silly jokes to keep them entertained.

I found out I was pregnant later that year and on a hot August day in 2002, Jules Alexander Nimmo made his entrance into the world. This time I was lucky enough to have a home water birth although it very nearly didn't happen. Andy slipped on the wet floor while trying to fill the birth pool and cracked his head. But it all worked out in the end and Jules was born in the early hours of the morning while his siblings slept in the next room and our cat purred nearby. Theo and Xanthe were delighted to run into our room when they woke up to meet their new baby brother. We knew we were expecting a boy: Theo had punched the air at the news and Xanthe had been disappointed (but that hadn't lasted long once I gave her the new Little Mermaid swimming costume I had bought her as compensation).

Jules was a perfect baby. He immediately fitted in, was gentle and quiet, walked early, but was very late to talk. It was now, with three children, that I decided to reduce my commuting time and find something closer to home. I took on the role of Head of Marketing and Student Support at a local college and we employed childminders and after-school nannies. Things were getting back on an even keel and we even felt that with

Jules we had a little bit of Dad back in the family. He was the spitting image of my father as a baby.

Andy turned forty and was riding his prized Harley-Davidson to work each day. Weekends were spent taking the older children to ballet, football and martial arts classes. We booked babysitters when we could; we had busy lives but we recognised that it would be easy to slip into the habit of not looking after our own relationship, so we tried to get out once a month to the cinema or for dinner, just to remember who we were. Once a year, we moved mountains to have a precious weekend away, just the two of us, even if our conversation did tend to steer back to the children and their growing needs.

My new role at the college was vastly different from my other roles working on either the client or agency side for blue chip firms, but it was incredibly rewarding to be in an education environment and even better not to be hopping on a plane every other week, or battling my way onto a packed commuter train.

Theo and Xanthe were both going to after-school clubs and Jules was with the lovely childminder who had also taken care of the older two. The kids would wait at the door as soon as they heard the gravelly roar of Andy's Harley-Davidson rounding the corner, anxious to tell Daddy all about their day.

It was perfect. Three happy, healthy children, two cats, a lovely home, rewarding careers. Andy had turned forty the year Jules was born. I was thirty-four.

Just one more.

I could not shake off the feeling of wanting to round off our family and have another. Four children was my dream.

"I'll go part time. We'll manage," I begged Andy.

Not that it took much persuasion. Andy had always felt

the same as me: the more the merrier. We had three, so why not four children? I, in turn, loved Andy for his 'let's go for it' attitude to life.

We were on a family holiday in Normandy in 2004 when I found out I was pregnant for the fourth time. Andy was thrilled. The baby was due around Valentine's Day 2005. Theo hoped that he or she would arrive on his birthday the week before.

But this time things felt different. Every pregnancy is unique but this time my symptoms were far worse. I just put it down to my age. This was baby number four. I had been twenty-eight years old when I was pregnant with Theo; I was now thirty-six. It shouldn't have come as a surprise to feel a lot more sick in the mornings and already show a sizeable bump, should it?

Andy wasn't going to come to the first, early dating scan. He was busy with work. It was difficult to shift commitments, but at the last minute he managed to get there. Time to see Nimmo Number Four on the big screen. Although we had done this three times before, we were just as excited. This was definitely our last child, so we wanted to savour the moment.

We breezed into the antenatal clinic. Andy, glancing at his watch, was mindful of the time because he had a meeting that afternoon. He was hoping to take along the scan pictures to show his client who had recently announced her pregnancy. But then the second nurse arrived with a harried expression on her face.

"According to our calculations your baby has a one-in-four risk of having Down's syndrome."

With those words, time stood still. I barely remember the rest of the conversation. We hugged and cried and then we went home. The nurse had given us an appointment to return in the next few days for a CVS test, to take a sample of amniotic fluid to confirm whether or not our baby had Down's.

That was it. There was no counselling, no information on bringing up a child with Down's. There was just an assumption that if the test was positive we would want to terminate. We did not know what we were going to do. We could barely process the information. My bump was already showing, we were about to go away on holiday with the children. I needed to know. We didn't know what we would do with any information we were given but I knew that the more facts I had, the easier it would be to try and work out a plan.

Andy, being a poker player, was, despite his shell-shock, pragmatic. "Well, one in four still gives us a seventy-five percent chance of the baby not having Down's," he reasoned.

I was told that if the test was positive I would need to book a termination as soon as possible. Overwhelmed and numb, we went home and phoned our parents to share the news. We tried to keep smiling in front of the children but it was hard; all I could think about was my three perfect children. What had we been thinking when we decided to have another when we already had a perfect family?

Two days after the scan, we returned to the hospital and I underwent the CVS procedure. The doctor showed us the little vial of fluid, which contained the information that would dictate the direction of our lives. There was a small risk of miscarrying following the procedure. What if, in the end, everything was fine with the baby and I miscarried anyway? This was hell. We gave the nurse our mobile numbers and she promised to call as soon as they had the results. We did not make any contingency plans to return. We did not know what to do.

Oblivious to our torment, the children were expecting to go on holiday, so we packed the car and drove to the ferry port and boarded our ferry. I stood on the deck and watched the coastline disappear, relieved as miles were put between us and our nightmare.

The phone rang as promised on the day the results were due and Andy took the call while I sat next to him, my heart pounding.

"It's negative!!!"

That was all we heard. Maybe she said something about being unable to test for all the possible causes for our increased risk markers. Who knows? The full genome had not been mapped at that point and there were hundreds of genetic diseases that doctors were unable to definitively test for. But we were ecstatic. The baby was okay. I quickly phoned the nurse again.

"Do you know the sex based on the DNA analysis?"

"It's a girl," came her response.

A while later, Xanthe pressed her ear to my rapidly expanding stomach and said, "I can hear my baby sister. Hello Daisy!"

How did she know that I was expecting a girl? We were going to call her Ophelia Rose but not if Xanthe had her way. Her baby sister had officially been named Daisy Rose and that was all there was to it.

I could now relax, and although this pregnancy felt different and I seemed to have the biggest bump in the world, I just assumed that this baby would be breaking with tradition and be big compared to the others. It was when colleagues started asking if I was expecting twins or whether I was going on maternity leave soon that I started thinking that maybe things weren't quite right. I was only five months pregnant but was struggling to fit into my old maternity clothes.

* * *

I finished work for the day and as my route home took me past the hospital, I decided to pop into the walk-in midwife clinic to get checked out. This bump was getting very uncomfortable. Was there a twin that hadn't been seen in the scans? Better to be safe than sorry. Little did I know that this would be the last time I would ever work in an office.

The scan showed that I had too much amniotic fluid, a condition called polyhydramnios. If my waters broke, there was a danger that the umbilical cord could prolapse, starving the baby of oxygen and putting me at risk of bleeding to death. And so it began: having barely been in hospital as an adult I was going to get to know those peeling magnolia walls uncomfortably well over the coming weeks and months.

I was given steroid injections to strengthen the baby's lungs in case she decided to arrive early and attempts were made to drain some of the fluid off, which resulted in lots of worrying contractions before the fluid built back up again.

I became anaemic. My liver had developed a rare pregnancy complication called obstetric cholestasis where bile acids were building up, causing unbearable itching. I couldn't eat or sleep and was the size of a house with all the fluid in my stomach.

This was definitely a very different pregnancy but I took comfort in the fact that all the baby's vital signs were good. Maybe it was just my body that wasn't coping with being pregnant this time?

CHAPTER SIX

"Mummy, can we post my Christmas list to Santa? I need to make sure he gets it."

Christmas was only a few weeks away. The children were beside themselves with excitement. At seven, five and two years old, they were in the midst of frantic preparations at school and nursery, making paper chains, rehearsing for their nativities, and looking forward to all the treats the festive season held in store.

Xanthe had requested a new dolly that would cry just like her baby sister. Theo was hoping for a bike now that he had outgrown his smaller one and learned to ride without stabilisers. Thank goodness for online shopping, which was starting to take off, meaning I was able to sort out the children's Christmas presents.

Every now and then I was allowed out of hospital to wrap presents and watch the children in their Christmas plays. They had no inkling that something was not right. They were too little to notice much, consumed with excitement at the prospect not only of Christmas but also the imminent arrival of a new sibling. We didn't realise how imminent.

I had reached thirty-three weeks. I had been in and out of early labour for weeks. Amniotic fluid had been drained only to return. I was huge and unable to eat or sleep (it was just too uncomfortable) and itching constantly from the obstetric cholestasis. I felt constantly exhausted due to the onset of anaemia.

The consultant decided enough was enough. They had scanned and scanned the baby and things were not adding up. The baby's body was out of proportion: she had a large abdomen but short legs, yet everything remained within normal limits. I still had much too much fluid but there was nothing to tell them that anything was seriously wrong with the baby.

It was not safe to induce labour with so much water on board. Instead it was agreed that I should have an elective caesarean. So much for my planned home water birth—this was going to be about as medicalised as it got. I was exhausted and ill and there was no way I could have safely gone through labour anyway. I was allowed to go home for the night. Andy's mum flew down from Scotland to look after the children and the next day we returned to the hospital.

Daisy Rose Nimmo was delivered by C-section at 9.30am on the 22nd December 2004. She was blue and bloated with fluid and the first words she heard from her father were, "Fucking hell". I had a brief moment after she had been resuscitated to stroke her head in the incubator but she was then swiftly taken to the neonatal intensive care unit and put on a non-invasive form of ventilation called a CPAP machine to help her breathe.

The doctors got to work assessing her, trying to figure out what was going on, as she was clearly unwell but no one knew why.

"The doctor says she's a dwarf," Andy told me when he

came back up to the postnatal ward where I had been left on my own, with no baby, listening to the other mums with their new-borns.

This comment was to be our first experience of the occasional crassness of doctors when they forget it's people's lives they are dealing with.

I expressed milk and attempted to sleep, unable to move properly because of the searing pain across my stomach now that the epidural had worn off. It was so different from my experience of Jules' calm, drug-free home water birth just two years earlier. Daisy was moved out of intensive care and onto the high dependency unit on Christmas Day. Andy was at home with the children and his mum. At least I had been able to wrap their presents and could picture their faces as they opened them. Without Skype or FaceTime, I only had my imagination and their happy voices as they chatted to me on the hospital phone.

It was a miserable Christmas, despite our fixed smiles. I was still recovering from a tough pregnancy and major surgery, and on top of that we were worried about our new daughter and desperately trying to keep upbeat and happy for the sake of the children back home. Andy brought my Christmas lunch up to me on a plate covered in tinfoil.

We went to visit Daisy in the neonatal unit, passing the nurses' staff room where they were tucking into a buffet brought in to compensate for having to work on Christmas Day. Xanthe brought her new doll up to show her sister. It was bigger than Daisy.

I walked into the neonatal unit on Boxing Day, clutching my meagre bottle of expressed breast milk, doing the post-caesarean shuffle. I looked up to see the entire team of doctors, nurses and admin staff crowded around a television, watching rolling news coverage. A huge tsunami had hit South East Asia—thousands of people were dead or missing and it was a global disaster of epic proportions. To me it felt like the world was coming to an end.

I was torn. I needed to be with my new and very poorly daughter but my other children and Andy needed me too. I left hospital a couple of days later, armed with the obligatory industrial-strength breast pump, unable to drive because of the caesarean, but most importantly without our new baby.

Leaving hospital without your new-born baby must be among the hardest things a mother has to face. Your hormones scream to hold your baby, your aching body is a reminder of having given birth, while the empty Moses basket is a symbol of your loss. But the hardship didn't end there. At this stage, we did not know that there was anything wrong with Daisy other than her prematurity. Yet, while the other thirty-three weekers were breezing their way through the neonatal unit, Daisy with her swollen stomach, her silent cries and her arched back didn't seem to be making any progress.

When you give birth to a child with a disability you go through a profound sense of mourning. Mourning for the child you thought you were going to have, the birth you had planned, the life you were hoping for. You have to adjust to a new child, not the one you expected. I wasn't even sure why I was mourning—but the difficult pregnancy, the caesarean birth, Daisy's prematurity—everything was so different from what I had experienced before.

Once Christmas and New Year was out of the way, Rachel, the neonatal consultant, asked me to come to her office for a chat. Andy was at home looking after the other children.

With no family nearby, we had already started dividing our roles, with me spending days in the hospital with Daisy while he cared for the younger children. We hadn't even begun to think about what would happen once his paternity leave and holiday entitlement ran out. I had six months' maternity leave ahead of me before I had to worry about anything.

"We think there's something going on with Daisy," said Rachel.

I liked this consultant (a good thing too as we were going to know her for a very long time). She was a similar age to me, her children were the same ages as mine too, she had gone to the local school and been taught by the indefatigable local nun, Sister Catherine.

In another life Rachel and I would have probably been friends. Instead, as it turned out, here she was, just back from maternity leave with her third child herself, telling me that she would like to call a geneticist in to examine Daisy.

"Yes, yes please," I responded.

There had to be a reason why Daisy was not doing as well as the other children coming in and out of the unit. At the time, however, I was blind to the subtle signs clinicians are trained to observe; her weak cry, the way she held her hands in what we now know is called ulnar deviation, her low-set ears and wide nasal bridge – Andy and I didn't see all this; we just saw our little girl.

"We are going to run a lot of tests, mainly aimed at eliminating possible diagnoses," Rachel explained.

"Yes, of course, that's fine," I said.

Andy and I worked with facts. We had no fear of tests: we just wanted to know what was going on in order to be able to formulate a plan. It was how we always operated.

"Lastly," she continued. "You are going to need a good relationship with your doctor. Is there a particular one you like to see?"

This is a note to all neonatologists, paediatricians, doctors and health professionals out there. This was joined-up thinking. This was from a mum who was not only a neonatologist but had been through the neonatal unit with her own babies. She understood that once you are out in the community you need a good relationship with your doctor (we didn't know how good at this point). Because of that single action and the line of communication that was opened between Daisy's consultant while she was still in hospital and our doctor at home, a multitude of issues were avoided.

There was a flurry of activity as armfuls of Daisy's blood were taken for specialised testing that very day. Scans and X-rays were scheduled, and then a few days later the geneticist appeared.

We did not know what time she would be arriving and Andy needed to get home to pick Theo and Xanthe up from school and Jules from the childminder. I was on my own when she came into the unit. Neonatal units do not afford much privacy for parents. You spend your days next to your child's incubator or cot, watching the clock so you can administer the next 'care' (i.e. change their nappy – we were learning the lingo), or give a milk feed through their nasal gastric tube, or watch the nurse give some medications.

Once the babies were stable, it was a waiting game, waiting for the baby to grow or waiting for them to be transferred to surgery. Sometimes I would come into the unit and an incubator would be gone—a baby had not made it through the night. Other times it was because they were well enough to go home. You knew that once you had progressed through the various rooms—intensive care, high dependency, special care—you were on the home straight. In Daisy's case, she spent a lot of time in special care.

Dr Stuart, the geneticist, was a softly spoken woman with a very strong regional Scots accent. Andy's family were from the West Coast of Scotland; I was used to their colloquialisms. I've been deaf in my right ear since having measles at the age of three, and this, coupled with the doctor's soft voice and the background noise of the unit, made it really difficult to understand her.

It was in this public forum, without the offer of a private room to talk things through, that the geneticist told me all about my daughter's dysmorphic features, her loose skin, the shape of her eyes. She told me Daisy may have the clinical manifestations of one of a group of very similar syndromes that were currently the subject of a lot of research. The syndromes were Noonan, Cardio-Facio-Cutaneous syndrome (or CFC) and Costello syndrome.

She said that with some of the clinical signs it looked possible Daisy had the latter but she couldn't be certain. She hoped not, as that syndrome had been associated with an elevated risk of cancer and an increased incidence of premature death amongst the children studied. There was no clinic test but only time would tell. She would send me a leaflet. And that was it.

Back at home, I fired up Google and started my search for information. I spent hours in the evenings researching Daisy's symptoms, trying to get answers. Later I would learn *not* to do this and to avoid Dr Google as my first port of call. Pictures of children and adults flashed up on my screen. No way was my beautiful baby going to look like that. I ran through the list of possible problems: *short stature, developmental delay, feeding difficulties, endocrine problems, orthopaedic manifestations, heart problems, increased risk of cancer*...the list was endless. I closed the computer down. We didn't know if she actually had Costello syndrome. She could have something treatable.

Already within the neonatal unit Daisy had a reputation for not sleeping, for crying all night. I walked in one morning and her cot wasn't there. I froze, knowing what that normally meant. But Daisy had been moved into another room as she was waking the other babies. She lay with her head arched back, her hands clasped to her chest, a nasal-gastric tube taped to her face, her stomach bloated. Scans showed she had swallowing problems, but no answers could be given to why her stomach was so bloated and intolerant to feeds. The initial array of tests Rachel ordered were negative, and we still had no answers.

Everyone scratched their heads. Why did I have so much amniotic fluid when pregnant with her? Why was she unable to take large volumes of milk feed? Why did she cry so much? Nothing added up.

CHAPTER SEVEN

"I'll give the hospital a miss today, keep things ticking over at home, sort out the children..."

An ambulance was called to take Daisy to the Royal Brompton Hospital in London for an echocardiogram to check her heart function. It had been ordered by the geneticist. Children with Costello syndrome can have heart problems and they wanted to see if there was anything going on with Daisy's heart.

As we snaked our way through the traffic-bound streets of South London, the nurse smiled and said, "How's your husband coping?"

"Fine," I replied with a fixed smile that British people do so well.

He was not fine. We were not fine. We were struggling to come to terms with everything that had happened over the previous few weeks and Andy was finding the daily visits to the neonatal unit, where our lives were on show, tough to handle.

I realised that the staff must have been talking about us and that they had noticed that Andy was not at the hospital as much as he had been in the early days. This was my first experience of the goldfish bowl, when your life is on display now that you have a child with a disability. We might not know what that disability was, but everyone would be watching us, party to information about our child, and by association, us.

"Fine," I repeated. "Well, you know...I mean..." I felt myself becoming tongue-tied. I didn't know this nurse. I didn't want to have to pour out all my feeling and emotions to her.

I was worried about Daisy, I was worried about Andy. I was worried about our other children. I was being pulled in so many directions.

I was no longer Steph. To the hospital staff I was 'Mum' to Daisy. To this day the label still grates. There are only four people in the world who can call me 'Mum', but this habit in paediatric care of not learning the parents' names and referring to them as 'Mum' and 'Dad' felt disempowering. Here I was with all my professional experience, responsible for multi-million pound budgets, two degrees, having travelled the world and managed multiple teams and yet my whole identity was now reduced to 'Mum'.

The heart tests showed a mild thickening of Daisy's cardiac muscle but nothing to be concerned about. The cardiologist wasn't worried. I wasn't worried. But little did we know that Daisy was already writing her own book: *Things To Be Concerned About*.

For the first two months of her life, all Daisy had known was bright hospital lighting, the beeping of monitors and plastic boxes masquerading as cots. She had gone from being cosy in my womb, bouncing around in an ocean of amniotic fluid, to being dragged out and having masks put over her face and tubes shoved into her.

But now the time had come to bed in, to take up residence in the parents' bedroom at the end of the corridor in preparation for taking Daisy home. I wheeled Daisy in her little plastic cot down to the bedroom with me after her evening meds and prepared to sleep. She cried all night and would not be consoled unless I held her and paced the corridors.

The seasons had changed since her birth: the Christmas decorations had come down, the tree outside the neonatal unit was showing green leaves. Spring was around the corner. Life had not stopped when we walked through these doors. We needed to get home.

Andy brought the children up to the hospital the next day. They raced around the parents' bedroom, over-excited, bored with the hospital and high on the sugary sweets we dished out to placate them. Andy and I were over-tired, stressed and worried. It showed in our faces and our short fuses with the children. It was grim.

Just a week past her due date we brought Daisy home, armed with medications and instructions and follow-up appointments. The last box to tick before leaving the unit was resuscitation training. Every parent leaving with a premature child is taught how to resuscitate a baby before they are allowed home. We bought the obligatory boxes of biscuits and chocolates and made cards with the children, thanking the hospital staff for their help, promising to return for a visit. We fixed the car seat in the back of the car and drove away.

Now we could get on with our lives. Away from the goldfish bowl. Now our family of five could properly become a family of six and we could get to know Daisy.

What if she was found to have this Costello syndrome the geneticist had talked about? Was that it? My life over? No more holidays, no more parties, no more fun?

I imagined Andy and me as that couple, the one with the

tired and pained expressions, holding the hand of an adult child as they made their way to the shops. Was this our life from now on? As grey and unpromising as the day outside?

We were mourning. Mourning for the future we thought we would have. The child we thought we would have. The dreams we had lost. And yet we had been given this new life. Daisy hadn't asked to be born; she needed us. My maternal instinct was as strong as ever, but I was sad. We could have walked away, we could have given up on her, but that was never up for consideration. I grieved for the life we once knew. That chapter was now closed.

Her brothers and sisters, on the other hand, were over the moon. They loved their new baby sister, even if she did have a tube up her nose for feeding. They just saw Daisy as Daisy and they talked about her all the time.

"Daisy loves me the most! Look how she's looking at me," Xanthe would announce in her high-pitched voice as she skipped around her sister's cot.

Theo would try and make her smile, despite the fact that she was only one week past her official due date by the time she came home.

Daisy still seemed so small and fragile compared to her siblings, and two-year-old Jules seemed like a giant in comparison. Her head was thrown back permanently. We were later to learn that her reflux and airway issues forced her to do this to try and be more comfortable. Daisy was rarely relaxed when we held her in our arms. Maybe having three little blonde heads all vying for her attention while I cuddled her made her stiffen up? Overwhelming sibling love was an understatement!

It was hard work. Jules was still only two, still just a baby,

Xanthe and Theo were in school and Andy was back at work. We were being pulled in so many directions but we were determined to be positive.

The nights were the worst. Daisy would cry, refusing to settle or be comforted, as she arched her back in pain, sweating, her skin grey. I could not get enough prescription milk into her and she was becoming dehydrated.

A month after we had been discharged from the neonatal unit, we took Daisy to the emergency department. She was clearly unwell. She was admitted onto the ward and we were then given the news that, judging by one of the blood tests, Daisy had very high markers (called catecholamines) in her blood for a neuro-endocrine tumour. There was a strong possibility that she had a malignant tumour, the doctors just did not know where.

I looked over at Andy and saw the pain in his eyes. Just as we were getting our heads around having a child with a disability, just as we had fallen in love with this feisty little fighter, was she going to be taken away from us? Had she fought so hard only to be snatched away so soon?

Daisy was transferred to Great Ormond Street Hospital and so began our long relationship with them. Everyone in the UK knows Great Ormond Street. It's a centre of excellence for children's medicine: they would sort Daisy out, they would make this all go away so that we could be a family again and have Daisy back.

Our first lesson about healthcare and medicine was a hard one. When it comes to the complexities of a rare disease, everything is academic guesswork. We had always expected the doctors to have the answers. They had let us down when my dad was ill but that was because of their poor communication, not because they did not know what was going on or how to manage it. Now that medicine had advanced and we were in the best children's hospital in the UK, we looked to the doctors to tell us what they were going to do and to give us a plan.

Every child is different; often there are no answers, often it's trial and error or watchful waiting. It was a tough lesson to learn. We found ourselves on an oncology ward in a newer part of the hospital with views of St Paul's Cathedral in the distance. The plan was for Daisy to have an urgent MRI scan.

An ultrasound had shown enlarged ventricles, the fluid filled areas in the brain, and the first thing was to rule out hydrocephalus, water on the brain. Because Daisy was so little she needed to be anaesthetised for the MRI. This added to the delays as she had to wait for a slot on the general anaesthetic list. Why couldn't they just do it? Could they not see how poorly she was becoming? Her body was arched into an almost 90-degree backbend at times. She was clearly distressed and in pain and it was unbearable to witness. But this was the hospital that treated some of the sickest children in the country. Here every child was a priority. We were becoming so frustrated as we embarked on our journey into the workings of the over-stretched National Health Service and paediatric care.

Andy had started bringing Jules to the ward and he would sleep on my camp bed next to Daisy's cot and play in the playroom until it was time to go home. We were relying on childminders, friends, our mothers (both of whom lived very far away), whoever we could find to step in and travel to London, as Andy tried to keep working.

Eventually Daisy had her MRI. It was all within normal limits and nothing showed up to explain her pain. The next step was a nuclear medicine scan to see if she had an occult or hidden neuroblastoma or another tumour that the ordinary scans could not pick up. Lots of specialist blood tests had been sent and these were going to take a while to come back.

The oncologist asked if the genetics team could come and review Daisy. After my first experience of meeting a geneticist I was very reticent to have any more conversations with anyone from genetics. But we owed it to Daisy to leave no stone unturned so I reluctantly agreed.

The Dutch professor who had recently taken up a role in the genetics team at the hospital specialised in dysmorphic syndromes, genetic conditions where physical differences in the face or body indicate the likelihood of a gene mutation. He had previously been at the University of Utrecht, which meant that I warmed to him because our good friends lived in Utrecht and we had enjoyed many happy times in Holland. He seemed very kind and caring.

He asked me if it was okay for him to describe what he saw to his team. He talked to Daisy and told me about other children he had met with Costello syndrome who were growing up to be very able. He said that it was likely that she did have the syndrome but the most important thing to remember was that she was Daisy, not a syndrome, not a diagnosis, just a little girl.

When he left the room, Daisy gave me her first ever smile, as if to say, *"It will be okay, Mum,"* and my heart soared.

CHAPTER EIGHT

"I have asked the intensive care outreach team to come and review Daisy's breathing, she's starting to struggle and I'm not happy."

Daisy's condition deteriorated over the next couple of days. Her breathing, which had always been loud and wheezy, was becoming worse and she was fighting for each breath. The on-call doctors and clinical site practitioners came to assess her and eventually it was decided that she would be taken into the intensive care unit (ICU). She was working too hard and becoming exhausted.

We raced along the corridors and Daisy was put on a ventilator to support her breathing. I went to bed exhausted. I had been awake with her continuously and could barely function. Now that she was in intensive care there was nothing I could do. They would call me if anything changed.

Things moved quickly in the paediatric ICU as specialist after specialist came in and each had a new bombshell for us: the cardiologists had found that she had increased thickening in her heart muscle, a condition called cardiomyopathy; the respiratory team wanted to take her to theatre to examine her airway; she had pneumonia and had aspirated milk feed into her lungs; and the gastroenterologists wanted to test her for reflux. I left the room (it was too overwhelming to try and process all this news in one go) but Andy stayed to hear all the updates.

Daisy went to theatre for an examination of her airway with a camera. She was found to have a floppy larynx, a condition called laryngomalacia, which accounted for the seriousness of her condition and why she had gone into respiratory distress.

She spent a week on a ventilator. During this time the oncology team came to speak to me: the specialist nuclear medicine scan, which had taken place while she was still ventilated, had not shown any evidence of tumours and the tests had come back negative, which was a huge relief. We were in the clear, for now.

However, the likelihood was that Daisy did have Costello syndrome, which meant she would need regular checks and monitoring as her risk of developing cancer was much higher than the general population. In a typical Costello syndrome double whammy, recent research had also found that tumour markers called catecholamines are raised in children with the syndrome, which can cause a false positive result. Daisy's tumour markers had been extraordinarily high because of the stress of her respiratory problems.

Our next stop was the neurology ward. Starfish Ward was in the old, Victorian part of the hospital, a huge contrast to the bright, modern oncology ward and intensive care unit. There were no en-suite bathrooms here, just one bathroom for parents and patients. There were no sunsets over St Paul's, just a dreary view over the ambulance bay and kitchens.

On the wall of the ward, however, was a beautifully illustrated picture of a boy throwing a starfish into the sea, and next to it was this story, adapted from an essay by the scientist Loren Eiseley:

Once upon a time, there was a wise man who used to go to the ocean to do his writing. He had a habit of walking on the beach before he began his work.

One day, as he was walking along the shore, he looked down the beach and saw a human figure moving like a dancer.

He smiled to himself at the thought of someone who would dance to the day, and so, he walked faster to catch up.

As he got closer, he noticed that the figure was that of a young man, and that what he was doing was not dancing at all. The young man was reaching down to the shore, picking up small objects, and throwing them into the ocean.

He came closer still and called out, "Good morning! May I ask what it is that you are doing?"

The young man paused, looked up, and replied, "Throwing starfish into the ocean."

"I must ask, then, why are you throwing starfish into the ocean?" asked the somewhat startled wise man.

To this, the young man replied, "The sun is up and the tide is going out. If I don't throw them in, they'll die."

Upon hearing this, the wise man commented, "But, young man, do you not realise that there are miles and miles of beach and there are starfish all along every mile? You can't possibly make a difference!"

At this, the young man bent down, picked up yet another starfish, and threw it into the ocean.

As it met the water, he said, "It made a difference for that one!"

We needed to be the difference. We needed to be strong for

Daisy and to fight for her to get the best out of life, however short that life was going to be.

The bad news kept coming.

Neurology tests had shown that Daisy was probably blind. The medical reason was severe nystagmus, a constant flickering of her eyes together with a delayed visually evoked response, as the signals from the eye to the back of the brain were not being processed efficiently.

We were devastated but in time we were to learn that the brain has an incredible capacity to rewire and make use of whatever information was available to it. As a result, Daisy's functional vision came to be a lot better than the tests had initially indicated. At the time, however, it just felt like yet another piece of bad news on top of all the other bad news we had been given.

Nearly three months after first leaving the ward, we transferred back to our local hospital with a nourished Daisy and an increased list of medications and diagnoses. We were six months down the line from that ordinary day when I had left my office to see the midwives as I was concerned things were not quite right. What a journey it had been.

I received two important letters during that time. The first was a letter from the genetics service. The gene mutation for Costello syndrome had been isolated as part of the genome mapping project and Daisy had tested positive for it. Her diagnosis was now certain. The second letter was from a children's hospice— our local team had referred Daisy there for respite breaks and support, and the referral had been accepted. In the space of two letters our lives had now been mapped out: Daisy was confirmed to have a life-limiting condition but at least, thanks to hospice support, we would not face this journey on our own.

Summer was around the corner, I savoured the flowering roses and longer evenings, and with it, memories of summers before the children, when we had driven to the South of France to visit Andy's friend Ben, a writer.

Andy had proposed to me on one of our previous summer holidays when we were carefree and time was spent with friends, drinking, laughing, eating, sunbathing and swimming. How oblivious we had been to the future and what it had in store.

CHAPTER NINE

"Can you believe it? Our baby girl is starting school today."

Daisy started school in September 2008. I was so excited that I forgot to take the obligatory first day of school photographs! At last, I had all four children in full-time education. There had once been a time when all I wanted was all four children to be in the same place, for Daisy to be taught by the same teachers who had taught her brothers and sister. Working with our early years support worker I began to realise it was not about me and my idealised view of our family, it was about what was right for Daisy.

As Daisy had been diagnosed with a severe visual impairment and registered as partially blind we were able to get funding for her to attend a specialist school for children with sensory issues, only three miles away from our home.

Daisy loved it, and the staff loved her. We were rapidly coming to realise that while we worried about Daisy's medical needs, whether people would accept her, what she was able to do, Daisy was just getting on with it. She called the shots with her winning smile and happy demeanour. People warmed to Daisy. She was such a character. Children with Costello syndrome have short stature but Daisy made up for her lack of height with her larger than life personality. She had an infectious smile, a halo of golden curls and a sophisticated sense of humour. She loved slapstick comedy and nothing made her dissolve into fits of giggles more than if someone tripped up or dropped something.

Daisy was permanently connected to a feed pump and this drip-fed a specialised prescription milk into her stomach twenty-four hours a day via a stomach tube called a gastrostomy. Daisy was now able to walk, so during school hours we would put the pump and milk into a little rucksack and Daisy's school helper would follow her holding the bag so that it did not become detached from the gastrostomy tube.

I began to get into a routine. A friend would pick up Xanthe and Jules as she passed my house every day and walk them to their primary school so that I could drop Daisy off at her school. Theo was now in senior school and making his own way there by bus and tube. I would rush to pick up Jules and Xanthe at the end of the day and battle through traffic to collect Daisy from her school near Wimbledon Village. I was just like any other mum doing the school run, frazzled but living a vaguely normal life at long last.

And yet Daisy's health issues remained problematic. Out of the blue she would start screaming for no reason. One day she kicked her foot out in pain, breaking a toe on a table leg in the process. I took her to the hospital's Accident & Emergency department (A&E), where the focus was on the broken toe and not *why* she had kicked out in the first place. During another visit to the hospital, when she was crying and in pain, a junior doctor suggested that she was perhaps teething. I was a mum of four. I knew the difference between teething pain and these incessant episodes. I just gritted my teeth and nodded.

And then things got bad, really bad. Daisy spiked a temperature and began vomiting. I took her to A&E again and this time a consultant who had known her from the neonatal unit was on duty. He was clearly worried and could see that there was so much more to this than a normal childhood illness. The decision was made to admit Daisy onto the children's ward.

As the porter pushed Daisy's trolley along the cold, white hospital corridors, I had the feeling that this stay was not going to be a short one. Instinctively, I knew that we would be in for the long haul.

Daisy went into hospital in early October. By early November she was still there. She had worryingly high infection markers in her blood, was pouring bile out of her stomach and could barely tolerate any of her feed. She needed intravenous fluids but her veins were so small and scarred that she required new cannulas to be inserted for IV access on a daily basis. I found it gruelling to watch the doctors hold her down to insert another line into whatever vein they could find. Daisy was losing weight fast and needed fluids to counteract the vomiting and diarrhoea. We were waiting for a bed to become available at Great Ormond Street so that she could have an exploratory endoscopy camera test and find a solution for more permanent access to her veins to avoid the stress of them collapsing and the need for the barbaric multiple cannulations.

I sat looking at Daisy, pale, limp, sunken-eyed from lack of fluids and nutrition and willed her to be the little girl who had been so excited to be going to school a few weeks previously.

At long last the call came and we were transferred to the gastrointestinal ward at Great Ormond Street. On the day of transfer Daisy spiked a forty-degree temperature and had a massive bout of bloody diarrhoea—we weren't moving a moment too soon.

Daisy had stayed on this ward for tests before, but this time it was different. There were a lot of new staff who did not know her, or us.

A great deal of our energy was spent fighting with junior doctors and other staff members who assumed that Daisy would be with them for a couple of days for tests, then shipped back to the local hospital. Our expectations and the ward manager's expectations were clearly very different and the saddest part was that with the focus on bed availability and talk of bed blocking, clinicians were losing sight of the most important fact: here was a desperately sick child on the ward who needed urgent care.

Daisy was clearly deteriorating and at last, after a month as an inpatient, countless cannulas and minimal nutrition, she went to theatre for endoscopies to try and identify what exactly was going on.

The gastroenterology consultant was waiting for us when we went to theatre to collect her. He had a stack of pictures in his hand, pictures of a raw, bleeding, infected gastrointestinal tract. Daisy had colitis—severe inflammation—from her oesophagus to her rectum. In some parts there were open ulcers. It was as bad as it could get. The pictures made me wince. How long had she been like this, in agony as we tried to increase her milk feed?

The plan was to take her back to theatre the next day and insert a permanent line into one of her main veins so that she could start intravenous nutrition. The doctors now needed to work out why her gut was so inflamed and to come up with a plan.

The following day Daisy had her first central line fitted. At least now, with a permanent line inserted into her chest, there would be no more traumatic cannula insertions.

At home the older children were desperately upset. While they understood that Daisy was very poorly and would be in hospital for quite a while, they needed me to be with them too, so I swapped shifts with Andy. Despite my guilt at leaving Daisy, it was bliss to be at home, giving the children their fish fingers, singing songs and getting wrapped up in the bath-time routine.

Andy was there on the evening of 5th November 2008 when Daisy's first ever bag of TPN—Total Parenteral Nutrition, the precise mixture of intravenous nutrition that would now keep her alive—was put up. We had clearly entered new territory with Daisy. Our research told us that this was not the normal pattern with Costello syndrome.

Up until that point, Daisy's care had been reasonably straightforward since the pump she needed to deliver her milk over twenty-four hours was pretty fool-proof and the risks were minimal. TPN, however, was in another league. Operating it was both a medical and technical procedure, and while the doctors hoped they could get Daisy to a position where she would not need it, I knew in my heart of hearts that at some point in the following year we would be going home with TPN.

The biggest risk to Daisy now was her central line, and we had been told that there were many possible complications associated with having a catheter permanently tunnelled into a main vein. By day two it was already making trouble. The heart monitor she was hooked up to showed that her heart rate was dipping to dangerously low levels; she was now having bradycardias, clinically dangerous low heart rates.

The cardiology team were called and after much head scratching someone had the bright idea to do an X-ray and check on the position of Daisy's central line. It had migrated into her heart, hence all the problems. Another trip to theatre followed, her third general anaesthetic that week alone.

The gastro doctors hoped that a period of total gut rest plus a very high dose of steroids and immunosuppressant therapy might help calm down the inflammation in Daisy's gastrointestinal tract releasing her from the need to be on TPN. We did not need to be in Great Ormond Street to put this plan into action and it was now vital that both Andy and I were close to home and providing some sort of stability for the other children. We were over the moon to be transferred back to our local hospital after two long and stressful weeks on the gastro ward.

Tucking Theo up in bed that night, arranging his teddies in a line, he told me that all he wanted for Christmas was *Daisy to be back home with us all*.

"I know, my love," I said, sad to know that, barring a miracle, there was no way we could make it happen.

High-dose steroids and immunosuppressants put Daisy at huge risk of infection and life-threatening sepsis. The central line into her chest, which was providing the nutrients to keep her alive while her intestinal system had failed, could also be deadly. We lived with the constant risk of a line infection.

Daisy had only been back at the local hospital for twenty-four hours when she spiked a sudden high fever and developed rigours, an uncontrollable shaking often associated with sepsis. Blood cultures showed that she was indeed septic. When the full results came back it showed that she had both MRSA and E. coli in her blood stream. She was desperately ill.

Things were not looking good. The doctors poured antibiotics into her in a bid to kill the bugs.

The bright red rifampicin infusions stained her tears red, her iron levels dropped and she needed blood transfusion after blood transfusion. I'd swiftly learned that the problem with central lines is that they are made of plastic, and bacteria loves to colonise plastic. The only way to give Daisy a fighting chance was to change her line.

Daisy was reasonably stable but only the chemical cocktail of drugs was keeping her this way. She could not be on them long term as they were highly toxic and slowly destroying her body, but without them she would develop overwhelming sepsis and probably die. The line needed to go and a temporary one put in its place.

Not for the first time, Andy and I were faced with making a decision that no parent should have to make. Great Ormond Street could fit her in for a line removal and temporary line insertion on Christmas Eve, but it would mean she would be there for Christmas.

We had been working with the medical team to transfer Daisy to the hospice in Guildford just for Christmas so that we could all be together for a couple of days and enjoy some precious family time. But Daisy's condition had deteriorated so rapidly over the past year that we had to decide whether to give up any plans for Christmas as a family in a desperate gamble for her health or to take the risk and make some precious memories together in the knowledge that this could be our last Christmas together.

At that point I broke down and cried in front of the doctors.

"This is not fair." My voice shook. "We've come so far with her and now there's an even bigger mountain to climb. How much more does she have to go through? Does this family have to go through?"

For a moment, I felt utterly overwhelmed by everything but, as always, talking it through with Andy, working out our options, enabled us to come to our decision.

Thankfully Daisy was reasonably stable with her current antibiotic regime and we decided that family time and memories were the priority. Our team of hospice and hospital nurses and doctors moved heaven and earth to enable us to take Daisy out of the hospital on her birthday and spend Christmas surrounded by torn wrapping paper and her family.

CHAPTER TEN

"Look Daisy! We're not in the hospital anymore."

Christmas had taken on more significance since Daisy's arrival and I felt I needed to make up for that first Christmas when we hadn't been able to be together as a family. So, despite waking up in hospital on her fourth birthday, Daisy was so excited when we opened the door of the ambulance and she realised she was not being transferred back to Great Ormond Street but to a place she loved. Far from being a sad place for the dying, Daisy's hospice was a happy place for the living. It was just that the children there had a little less time for living than other children did.

Theo, Xanthe and Jules were beside themselves, thrilled to have Mummy and Daddy back and to have their sister out of hospital, albeit for just a few days. It was the best present ever. We were so grateful to our hospice nurses who had fought hard to convince the hospital doctors and Daisy's medical teams that the priority was to give our family some space and time to make memories.

Daisy needed that downtime as much as we did. While the

nurses managed all the complicated infusions and putting up her drips, she was able to just play, to be a little girl and forget about what had happened to her over the past few months. It gave her the mental strength to cope with the challenges ahead.

Daisy returned to Great Ormond Street in the new year and had the infected central line removed and a new line inserted. But still the cycle of infection and sepsis continued.

Daisy's intestines were so broken that bacteria were translocating into her blood stream and causing her to be desperately ill.

No decisions could be made about coming off TPN or coming home until Daisy was stable—but when were we ever going to get to that point? Life was a game of snakes and ladders. It was two steps forward and one step back. We cleared the MRSA from Daisy's line and then it became colonised with candida.

January became February and I began to make plans for Theo's twelfth birthday.

"Theo says there's a new Sonic the Hedgehog game coming out on PlayStation," I told Andy. "I think it's out at the same time as his birthday and he really wants it."

"OK, I'm on the case," he sighed, as he fired up the laptop to order it.

Once again, our hospice had come good and building on the successful Christmas escape, we were hoping to spend Theo's birthday weekend back in Guildford.

The week had started with snow, which really lifted everyone's spirits as school was cancelled. Even Daisy enjoyed looking at (if not touching) the bowl of snow the nurses brought into her room for her.

Theo, Xanthe, Jules and I walked the three miles to the

hospital in our wellies, laughing and throwing snowballs at each other. We spent the day in Daisy's room, which was surprisingly manageable with four very excited children in one confined space.

Towards the end of the week Daisy was quite clingy and pale. I was starting to become a parent expert, understanding many of the subtle signs that might indicate a problem with Daisy, I kept meaning to ask the doctors what her haemoglobin level was as I'd wondered if she was at the point of needing another blood transfusion. If that was the case, it would give her a boost, ready for our weekend at the hospice.

Once again, Daisy, or rather the bacteria running rampage throughout her system, called the shots. Within a few hours, Daisy deteriorated with sepsis—it came on that quickly. I took one look at her and called Andy at his office immediately.

"Drop everything," I said. "She's not looking good. Get here as soon as you can."

I had learned very early in my journey with Daisy that a good network of friends was crucial for survival, not just as moral support but also as practical support. Our nearest family members were at least three hours' drive away but our local friends were there for us day and night. It wasn't unusual for them to scoop up the older children and take care of them, keeping them safe while we focused on Daisy.

This was the first time I'd looked at my daughter and thought, *she's not going to make it.* She was shutting down, overcome with septic shock. An anaesthetist was bleeped to intubate her and the search began for a paediatric ICU bed.

It was Friday night and snowing, roads were in chaos and major motorways closed. There was no bed at Great Ormond Street. At one point Manchester was mentioned, with an air ambulance transfer in atrocious conditions. Eventually a bed was found in St George's Hospital, ten minutes by blue light down the road. A dopamine infusion was started and, when the paediatric intensive care transfer team arrived, noradrenaline was added to the mix. This seemed to do the trick and suddenly she turned the corner and we dared to breathe a tiny sigh of relief.

Leaving Daisy in the intensive care ward the next day, Andy and I took Theo and his siblings out for a birthday brunch, fixing smiles on our faces and trying not to show them how stressed and worried we were.

It is astonishing how one perfects the skills of leaping from one situation to another, moving from the surreal events of the previous night where Daisy had been so near death, to discussing Theo's theories on what was happening in the latest episode of Doctor Who.

The seasons changed again and while the other three children were busy with homework, after school clubs and playdates, Daisy remained an inpatient, boomeranging between her specialist hospital in central London and then back to our local hospital.

All the while Andy and I were parenting by rota. He would work in town and often come to the hospital straight afterwards so that I could get home and spend some time with our other children, who had forgotten what it was like to have two parents at home at the same time. I would return that evening to sleep in the bed next to Daisy and sometimes—when exhaustion and stress and sleep deprivation was too much—Andy would stay at the hospital and return to work the next day. His colleagues were none the wiser to the fact that staying overnight in Bloomsbury actually meant a camp bed with a plastic-covered mattress on a children's ward in Great Ormond Street.

Eventually the decision was made that Daisy would be coming home on TPN. The doctors confirmed that she had intestinal failure and, despite their best efforts, her intestinal system was never going to work properly again. Caring for a child as complex as Daisy really was academic guesswork and the doctors did not have all the answers, but we trusted them and were, as always, in Daisy's hands.

The wheels were set in motion to commission everything involved in providing intravenous nutrition at home. Our house was checked to make sure it was suitable for a child who was immunosuppressed and dependent on intravenous nutrition. Fortunately, it was (there wasn't a plan B). Boxes and equipment started to arrive, a large fridge to store the bags of fluids (specially compounded to Daisy's precise needs and delivered weekly), boxes of syringes, alcohol wipes, gloves, sharps bins for discarded needles and drug ampoules. Faced with the paraphernalia of a hospital treatment room, our house was becoming medicalised as never before.

And then there was the training. In order for us to bring Daisy home, Andy and I had to be signed off as competent in her care, which involved a two-week intensive training programme where we learned everything there was to know about caring for a central line and administering intravenous fluids at home.

Day one of the training was trolley cleaning. Germ warfare. We really were starting at the beginning. As the days progressed we got to practice dressing changes on a plastic model, taking bloods and all the other essential practices needed to bring Daisy safely home. We learned about what could go wrong, the risks that living with a central line posed. Of course, we had seen many of these hazards already while Daisy was in hospital and we were only too aware of the knife-edge we were living on. It really was a matter of life and death for our daughter.

Like enthusiastic students we worked hard and studied our notes, knowing that we would only be able to bring Daisy home once we had passed the final test–the live connection. It's all very well learning about setting up an IV on a plastic model or watching a DVD, but it's something else to set up your own child's IV for the first time knowing that one mistake could be fatal.

I have sat many high-stakes exams over the years and spoken at major conferences. Andy had appeared in front of huge audiences. But nothing is as scary as performing a medical procedure on your own child while a nurse watches and assesses you. If you get one step wrong, you will not be signed off and it will delay your child's homecoming.

Daisy was so patient with us. From day one she knew that her central line was special. This was her lifeline. She never pulled it or interfered with it. Instead she watched and waited while we put up her TPN and IVs, knowing that this kept her safe and alive.

Both Andy and I were signed off to administer Daisy's TPN and, at long last, ten months after being first admitted to hospital, Daisy–our beloved daughter–came home.

She was a different child to the Daisy who had been admitted to hospital all those months previously, and we were different parents. The months had taken their toll. Staring death in the face, making huge, life-changing decisions, seeing Daisy struggle with pain, our older children having to cope with absentee parents and unpredictable routines, our family fragmented, we left hospital a changed family but happy to be together at last under the same roof, despite all of the equipment, the worry and the workload.

We lasted eighteen days before Daisy was admitted again. She had deteriorated overnight with high temperatures and once again the doctors were querying whether her central line was infected.

In all, apart from those eighteen days at home, Daisy ended up spending twelve months in hospital between 2008 and 2009. We nearly lost her on several occasions. We had to learn new skills to keep her alive and with us, but by the end of 2009 we were once again trying to retain some sense of normality as we juggled Daisy's quadrupled care needs with the increasing needs of our other children who were also struggling with their own normal, growing-up issues.

I looked at pictures of the older three children, taken before Daisy's arrival. They were running around on the beach, Jules taking his first tottering steps before falling into the wet sand with a bemused look on his face, Theo frantically digging holes and building sandcastles, Xanthe practicing cartwheels and handstands. The children seemed so carefree and happy.

Theo had moved up to high school, a tough enough transition at any time without the added burden of absentee parents and a poorly sister. He seemed to have a perpetual worried look on his face.

Xanthe was being bounced between after school clubs and activities when often all she really wanted was to be at home, her ever present sketchbook in her hand, surrounded by her own things. She was a popular girl with her long blonde hair and her talent for art and drama, and her creativity became an outlet for her to express her emotions.

Little Jules, with his August birthday, was the youngest in his year, he was navigating his way through primary school often not knowing which friend or neighbour would be collecting him at the end of the day, trying to be brave but clearly fed up with the unpredictability of his home life. Unlike his older two siblings, Jules had no memory of life before Daisy, but he saw that his friends did not have to spend hours over the weekend stuck in hospital wards or away from home, and he knew that things were very different in our family compared to his peers.

So much had happened in our lives in an incredibly short time, we were surviving on adrenaline, trying to keep things on an even keel for the older three children. We tried as much as possible to protect them and make time for them, I was acutely aware that they only had one shot at childhood.

Then there was Andy's history with depression; his medication helped but I needed to ensure that he did not hit rock bottom again. My life was a constant round of plate spinning, trying to keep everyone going, wondering how long I could keep this up myself.

My family was far away in Wales, Andy's in Scotland and it was difficult for them to come and visit and help out, so we were very much on our own. For me, the one who was trying to hold the family together and keep us from falling apart, life could get very lonely at times. I saw friends and family enjoying the normal family things, the things that I would never again take for granted, and I wondered if I would ever have that time again.

CHAPTER ELEVEN

"Steph, we need to start living in the moment, enjoying the view, not worrying about the future."

Bringing Daisy home on TPN wasn't the end of our problems. It didn't provide a miracle cure. Rather, it gave her nourishment and kept her alive, but she still faced an army of problems. Pain was a big issue, as well as the ever-present risk of sepsis. The visits to A&E, the calls to the London Ambulance Service, these became a routine part of our life and in between the adrenaline rush of medical emergencies, we continued to try and find our new kind of normal.

For a while after Daisy was born, we had worried and fretted about the future, trying to anticipate what would happen next, bracing ourselves for the next impact. Andy said we had been living as if we were in a car knowing it was going to crash, but not knowing when or where. While we were anticipating the crash, we were missing the beautiful views outside the window. There came a point where we just decided to unbuckle our seat belts and enjoy the ride. This attitude was to serve us well now that we were at home with yet another set of unknowns to contend with.

In many ways, I am grateful that everything happened gradually, bit by bit, layer by layer. We just rode the rollercoaster, seat belts off, going with the flow and taking each change as it came. This way we took it all in our stride and assimilated each new challenge into our lives. We rarely had the chance to stand still and reflect on what had happened since Daisy had been born. Even during the rare moments when she was stable, our growing family's needs filled all our time. There was no time to think about what we did not have, we could only focus on the here and now.

Life was moving on. Our children were growing up. I'd barely had time to enjoy time with Jules before Daisy was born and, consequently, his life had revolved around hospitals from the age of two.

I felt I had missed so many of his milestones. He had gone from a beautiful, perfect, compliant baby to a rough-and-tumble blond bombshell. The youngest in his year, he struggled at school. I'd assumed that his lack of academic progress was down to our unsettled home life. I did not worry about him too much though; he was, despite everything, a happy boy, always ready with a cuddle and two older siblings who would always have his back. He'd had to grow up so quickly but despite it all, he was content.

Xanthe was supported by a wonderful group of friends; she was becoming feisty and resilient and never stopped talking. In fact I can see her now, a tiny thing on the screen during my three-month scan, opening and closing her mouth. The Welsh call it 'chopsy'.

Xanthe was developing her own style, which I admired. Her artistic talent was shining through and it was clear that she was going to be her own unique person. She adored her little sister and lavished her with affection. Like me, she was practical. In the neonatal unit while the boys were wrestling on the floor, she sat helping with Daisy's tube feeds.

She was confident and independent, and although she worried about Daisy, again, just like me, she could switch her focus and banish the worry. Certainly her artistic talents helped communicate her feelings and her painting and drawing, together with her busy social life, were already outlets for managing a stressful home life.

Theo had been seven when Daisy was born. He was nearly four when my dad died and nearly six when his godmother, whom he affectionately called Granny Betty, died. He had already experienced a lot more than most children his age and had clear memories of a life before Daisy.

We joke that Theo was born awkward, but in a sense, it was true. After a very long, extended labour, he was eventually delivered with his hand on his head. In fact our first introduction to Great Ormond Street had been when Theo was eleven months old and he had an operation on his eye to open up the tear duct, which had been squashed at birth.

Theo was clearly a very intelligent little boy: he was in the Gifted and Talented stream in school, excelled in his tests and had an IQ well above the average for his age. But he worried us. He was bullied in school, called a geek for his love of all things Doctor Who-related when the rest of the boys were discussing football, and was sensitive and philosophical. He had two left feet and the idea of sport left him cold.

Being our first born, we had nothing to compare against. We lived in London, far away from extended family, and our friends were, like us, just starting families. It was only when Xanthe came along that we realised what hard work Theo was.

Theo continued to take up a lot of our time and attention. Daisy's needs were, in comparison, more straightforward. We would find ourselves exasperated with Theo, constantly shouting at him, telling him off, developing reward charts or systems to try and manage the outbursts, naughtiness and disruption he caused.

What we know now that we didn't know then was that he has high-functioning autism. Theo, put simply, is wired differently. He processes information differently. He views the world through a different lens to neurotypical people. I describe it as like having a different computer operating system; Theo is like a Mac whereas neurotypical people are like PCs. You can't operate a Mac in the same way as a PC.

With Daisy's arrival, Theo's world had been turned upside down. As a boy with high-functioning autism, he craved order, routine, stability. Yet, we were in and out of hospital with Daisy. Unable to make plans, we had to constantly change things and routine went out of the window. Everything you read about parenting a boy with autism tells you to have structure, to communicate what you are doing and stick to the plan. Poor Theo. At a time when his autism traits were shifting from quirky habits into problems that would affect his education and social skills, his comfort blanket—domestic familiarity and routine—was taken away from him.

We put Theo's behaviour and reactions down to worry and stress. It had crossed our minds that he might be dyspraxic; he is left handed, he was not good at sport, his presentation was appalling, and he had problems with buttons and shoelaces.

His teachers told us, again and again, that *"he needs to concentrate, he needs to focus, he needs to improve his handwriting."* No one stood back and looked at his behavioural traits and pieced them together. The negative remarks had a profound effect on his self-esteem and put him at the mercy of bullies able to exploit his weaknesses.

This inevitably led to a lot of outbursts, meltdowns and anxieties which, again, were labelled as naughtiness—he would be told off for not paying attention in front of the rest of the class and would burst into tears, making him even more vulnerable to bullies. We, in turn, would tell him to "*man up*", and there was liberal use of the naughty step, time-out room and removing of privileges following the advice of TV's Supernanny and all the other so-called parenting experts.

It's all very well telling a boy off for doing wrong, but what if they don't understand what they have done wrong? What if rocking on the back of their school chair or getting up to walk around the classroom when everyone else is sitting doing work is their way of dealing with over-stimulation and simply trying to still their mind? How confusing to be told that this is naughty when you have no control over your actions.

Theo passed the entrance exams to all our local grammar schools and we chose a school with a reputation for discipline. We realised he needed structure and boundaries—which he does. But what we also came to learn is that he needs people with the emotional intelligence to see beyond the behaviour and understand the whys.

The first few years of high school were very difficult. Theo went from being a high-flying, grade A student to falling into the lower sets. His grades slipped and he kept getting detentions for bad behaviour. We despaired. We knew there was more to it than met the eye. Theo was an inherently good boy; he was enthusiastic, polite, well-mannered. What we were coming to realise was that he was stressed, panicking, feeling out of control. As he describes it, *"There are times when there is just a whirring in my head"*. He started to develop very bad migraine headaches and miss school.

Not only were we taking phone calls from irate housemasters while in Great Ormond Street, but we were shouting at Theo for letting us down. It was truly an awful time, especially for Theo, who was going through incredible stress and anxiety but didn't know how to communicate what, at the time, went undiagnosed.

Andy and I were becoming exasperated as we tried our best to help Theo while remaining in the dark. We would swap shifts at the hospital, exhausted, needing a peaceful night off at home but instead having to deal with Theo's meltdowns and frustrations, winding the other two children up, refusing to go to bed, refusing to help out with chores. Wherever we turned there was a situation to be dealt with.

Home was not a respite and hospital with Daisy had its own issues. Whenever we had the chance, Andy and I would try and arrange sleepovers for our older children, and when a nurse we liked and trusted was on duty we would go out to dinner or to the local pub, just to reclaim some valuable time together.

Daisy had been on TPN for two years when it was decided that she should have an ileostomy stoma performed by her surgeons. The aim would be to put her colon out of action and see if diverting all her waste products into a stoma bag that she would wear on her stomach might help with the management of her pain. Another long hospital stay and recuperation ensued and another new skill for Andy and me to learn as we adapted to caring for a child with a stoma bag.

We were all hugely cheered up by the news, however, that our family had been chosen by a charity as one of only 20 in the UK to travel to Disney World in Florida with a team of medics and nurses to support us.

Now that Daisy was on TPN with far more complicated medical needs, not to mention the new stoma, there was no realistic way we could manage a big trip without a support team in tow.

In 2007 we had managed to take the whole family on our own to the Pacific Northwest in the US for the biennial Costello syndrome conference. So much had changed since then. But to go to Disney? We knew that it was something that we needed to do for the family, to create happy memories together. Things were deteriorating with Daisy. She was already life-limited. Going to Florida, especially as part of a supported group, would give the whole family a much-needed lift.

* * *

A meltdown is a term frequently used to describe the episodes that children with autism have when things get too much and they just can't cope. For Theo, the trigger was our trip to Disney World in Florida. In hindsight, it was a perfect storm waiting to happen.

We were travelling with 20 other families and support workers. It was a long-haul flight and we were uncertain about what we would find on our arrival. The overstimulation, the excitement about the Disney experience, the panic about not leaving behind vital medical supplies, our worry that this was a special dream trip for life-limited children and their families and the significance of that, our worry about the other children being okay—all of these things provided the ideal recipe for something to go seriously wrong.

Theo had a major panic attack and would not, could not, get into the car to go to the airport. For once, instead of shouting at him and telling him he was being selfish and letting us down, the penny dropped—and we realised that he was scared and feeling out of control.

All he wanted was a hug (if he would let us), reassurance and words of support.

Everything's going to be alright, Theo.

Our trip to Disney was wonderful. The Florida sunshine, even in November, warmed our spirits. It was hard work, juggling Daisy's TPN and fluids around the flight and different time zone but she was still able to have time off her TPN during the day and a milk feed via a pump connected to her jejunostomy tube at the top of her intestine.

Now that we'd had our lightbulb moment about Theo, Andy and I managed to relax more with him, which meant he relaxed, and he and Andy discovered a mutual love of rollercoasters and adrenaline rides.

We returned to the UK, batteries recharged, armed with souvenirs and hundreds of happy photos, determined to make things better for Theo.

CHAPTER TWELVE

"Theo has a neurodevelopmental condition called Asperger Syndrome, it's sometimes known as High Functioning Autism."

We arranged a private consultation with a neurodevelopmental specialist. Theo was thirteen years old. He needed support, especially in school. His work was spiralling as he headed down towards the bottom set. Theo's autism diagnosis opened doors to the support he needed. He was referred to Child and Adolescent Mental Health Services and in an extraordinary turn of good fortune was able to receive regular sessions with a counsellor with whom he immediately clicked.

We fought hard to get funding for additional support at Theo's school and soon the pieces started to fall into place. Theo felt he was being listened to; at long last he had people around who understood him.

We didn't get it right all of the time and the outbursts and meltdowns didn't disappear overnight, but we really worked hard to imagine ourselves in Theo's shoes and see the world through his eyes. Sometimes when we felt overwhelmed trying to support Theo in new ways, Andy and I would just lock ourselves in another room and chant our mantra, *"It's not us, it's the autism"*.

While caring for Daisy was hard work physically, caring for Theo was in many ways harder emotionally. Daisy's disabilities were obvious and extreme and we knew what the long-term outcome would be. For Theo, however, we'd had to reassess our expectations. There had been a time where we had thought he would be an A-star student and go to university, but our educational system was no match for his complex brain. He had a really high IQ, but lacked the focus needed to pass exams and sit in classrooms, a point he made when he walked out of class in the first term of sixth form and appeared in Daisy's hospital room announcing he had left school.

I just sighed and fired up Google: *options for highly intelligent boys who refuse to go down the traditional education route.*

We adjusted our sails again as we re-learned the language of autism. We had two children with diagnoses of additional needs, vastly different from one another, but equally needy.

Daisy had by now been diagnosed with a neuropathic bladder, it was retaining urine and causing spasms which explained her pain. It was not a complete surprise. We knew from the full thickness biopsy taken from her colon that her nerves were not functioning as they should and that this was contributing to her pain; often bladder problems go hand in hand with intestinal problems. In addition, the colon that had essentially been taken out of service when Daisy had her ileostomy formed was inflamed and bleeding. She was on large doses of steroids and immunosuppressant therapy and these were causing countless infections. It was a vicious cycle.

Hearing your child scream with pain at night is more than unbearable, it's gut wrenching. But when it's night after night and they still manage to get up the next day smiling and ready to go to school it moves from being a wrench to a part of life.

If it was one of my other children, the level of pain would have seemed unacceptable, but Daisy had experienced so much from day one that we had assimilated her experience into our lives.

A professor from a paediatric intestinal failure centre in the United States was visiting the hospital during one of Daisy's long admissions and her gastro consultant asked him to come and review her. The professor told me that, far from having a higher pain threshold, children who have chronic, ongoing pain issues feel it more intensely.

"It's like beating a path through the jungle," he explained. "The more you use that pathway the easier it is to navigate your way through the undergrowth and the quicker you reach your destination.

"It's the same with pain pathways. With constant pain the neurons carrying the pain sensors become more efficient at moving along to the nerve endings."

"So, what you are saying is that as Daisy is in constant pain she feels it more intensely? This whole building up tolerance to pain is a myth really?" I said.

The only solution was to take away the pain source, in this case Daisy's dysfunctional colon, but even that had no guarantee of success. It was unacceptable.

In hindsight I can reflect on why I didn't scream and shout and batter down the doctor's door, but that's not how it works when your child is so complex. It's about dogged persistence, making sure your child is on everyone's radar, leaving no stone unturned.

Eventually it was decided that it was time for another big surgery. The potential benefit of removing Daisy's colon outweighed the risk of the surgery not working, she could not go on as she was.

Daisy was scheduled for removal of her colon and at the same time the surgeons decided that her redundant appendix would be used to create a channel from her abdomen to her bladder called a mitrofanoff stoma. This, in theory, would make catheterising her bladder a little more straightforward.

After yet another ground-breaking surgery at Great Ormond Street Daisy bounced back incredibly well and in record time. Clearly the removal of that toxic, broken colon was the answer as her pain reduced and we could wean down some of the steroids and immunosuppressants that were also putting her at such risk of infection.

The decision to put Daisy through a mammoth, eight-hour surgical procedure with no guarantees that it would make a difference was not one that Andy and I took lightly. In fact, the operation had the potential to make her worse and carried the risk of ending her life on the operating table.

There had been numerous times when we had to think about what the right thing to do for Daisy was, and whether her pain and distress justified the chance of making her better. In this case our judgment was spot on and we were all relieved, particularly Daisy's wonderful surgeon, by the success of the operation.

Jules had recently started in the first year of high school. Jules had been so excited to move up to senior school, he couldn't wait to get into the big science labs and to meet new friends. He looked so tiny going off in his room-for-growth blazer with the huge school bag over his shoulder and shiny black shoes.

Within weeks, things began to break down. We knew that being the youngest in the year was not going to help him adapt to this huge change, but we knew that Jules was determined to do well. And then the homework slips started coming in: reports for missed homework, incomplete homework. Jules got a school record for the highest number of report slips in a week. And his bubble burst. He went from the happy, excited boy, keen to go to high school, to a surly, sad child with a bowed head.

Then came the detentions and the phone calls from the housemaster. This was becoming all too familiar. Almost as soon as I had hit 'send' on an email articulating my worries to the special needs co-ordinator at the school, a similar email arrived back. Our emails had crossed in the ether and we both had the same thought: did Jules also have some sort of additional need not explained by his age or birth order?

Now knowing what we did about Theo, it seemed impossible that Jules, who was and is very different, could have the same diagnosis. He didn't have the same obsessions, although there were obsessions of his own: space, planes, military things.

Yet the more we thought about it, the clearer it all became. The avoidance strategies in junior school, the late development of his speech, the difficulties organising himself for school, getting into fights as he misread social situations with his peers.

Again, we scrabbled together our finances and brought in a private psychologist. We were incredibly shocked when Jules was diagnosed with autism spectrum disorder as well. Once again the pieces were falling into place, just as Jules was falling apart.

School became overwhelming. He could not cope with the overload of information and commands. Puberty was around the corner together with its kryptonite hormones and he was sinking, totally disengaged with academia.

I had considered a specialist setting for Theo when he was diagnosed but he had point blank refused to consider a move from his high school, and given his high IQ he was able to gain some good qualifications with the minimum of work and maximum support and input from the learning support team.

It was different for Jules. His issues sat on a different part of the spectrum. He was struggling with anxiety and clearly the strategies that he employed as a little boy in his local, cosy junior school had failed him. Eventually Jules just refused to go to school.

And so, just as I had done a few years previously, I started researching specialist schools where my boy would feel safe. Much as I would have preferred Jules to find his own level and develop at his own pace, I was also acutely aware that to be able to do what he wanted in life he would need those all-important GCSE qualifications. So I steeled myself for the bureaucratic battle to move Jules to a specialist school with the support he needed to succeed.

Three children with additional needs, all very different, all with different demands on my increasingly-limited time and one typical teenager who needed me just as much as the others, maybe even more so.

Andy and I were juggling more than ever. While Daisy's needs tended to be practical, setting up her intravenous meds and TPN, changing her stoma bag and catheters, the boys needed emotional support to avoid descending into black moods or meltdowns that even Andy's extensive coaching skills couldn't always navigate. We were spinning plates, parenting by rota. If I was in Daisy's room managing her care, Andy would be downstairs cooking a meal after a busy day working with clients.

It was parenting at its most extreme and although life was completely full on, we still made time for each other, appreciating more than ever those little things: watching a film on the sofa together, a meal out when Daisy was in respite at the hospice, a brief conversation, a laugh. Incredibly we became stronger as a couple, determined to do the best by our children and enjoy life, no matter what it threw at us.

CHAPTER THIRTEEN

"It's not the cards you're dealt, it's how you play them."

This was one of Andy's favourite sayings.

Our children had one chance at childhood, however long, short or complicated that childhood was going to be, and we needed to make sure we were in the best position, both as a couple and as individuals, to get it right for our family.

Our lives were so different from those days when I travelled the world, managing global teams and huge marketing budgets. The day I had left my desk to visit the midwife in November 2004 seemed a lifetime ago.

My identity was no longer that of a marketing professional and working mother, I was now a carer, a full time mother, a stay at home mum. None of this had ever been on my life radar but I was still determined to make it work and do my best in the situation in which I now found myself. I was older, I had life experience, I had spent time being a 'normal' mum, I was going to make sure that we would make the best of our situation and make it work for our family.

Andy had taken voluntary redundancy from his company

and had set up on his own. Being his own boss meant that he could be a lot more flexible with his work hours and travelling.

We built an office at the end of our garden, referring to it as his International Headquarters. This increased flexibility meant we could spend more time together as a couple, which was so important when our children and our complex lives were pulling us in every direction.

We made the most of living in London, visiting an exhibition and fitting in lunch while the children were at school. Life was about seizing the moment, enjoying the small things, being spontaneous.

We had seen so many relationships fall apart with the stress of caring for a child with complex needs. We had been through too much as a couple to allow this to happen to us. We were stronger together, best friends and a formidable team.

It was not about the grand gestures; it was about the little things that you take for granted until they are taken away from you. During Daisy's long hospitalisations we craved normal time together to sit on the sofa, watch some rubbish TV, share a bottle of wine, go for a walk on Wimbledon common.

So often we would be like ships passing in the night, while one of us stayed with Daisy in hospital and the other held things together at home. We made time whenever we could so that our relationship stayed strong, even if we could not spend as much time together as we wanted anymore.

We were both in our forties and I was acutely aware that we needed to be strong, physically as well as mentally, to survive our current lifestyle demands. I knew that I could not keep going on microwave meals and toast in hospital. The glasses of Rioja in the pub with my other hospital mum friends were becoming a little too frequent. We would sneak out after dark while our children were inpatients, our phones ready in case we were called back to the hospital, quickly downing a few glasses in the local pub while comparing notes on the day.

Andy took a picture of me one day during one of our walks in the local park. I looked tired and my hair was a mess. I looked like I had not eaten fresh food all year. I did not want my forties to be like this, but it was a slippery slope.

Despite our circumstances, I did not want to become a mum who let herself go, who stood outside the hospital in her pyjamas, who was always late for the school run, who piled on the pounds with middle-age spread. This was not going to make me happy and for my children to be happy, I had to remember who I was. I was Andy's wife, Daisy's mum, Theo, Xanthe and Jules' mum, but I was also me and I needed to recapture that.

Even when pregnant with Theo I had promised that I was not going to be a frumpy mummy. Alongside my hospital bag I had carefully chosen a nice outfit to leave hospital in, a deliberate move away from my baggy maternity clothes.

I left hospital as a new mother as I had planned, immaculately dressed with my hair done and makeup on, but with the addition of a pair of fluffy slippers. Andy had left my shoes by the front door in his hurry to come and pick us up.

Thanks to my dad's love of running, I had always enjoyed exercise. Dad had been a great role model. Running was never a chore but I had fallen out of the habit of exercising regularly.

One cold, sleety, January day, I decided to put on my running shoes and get out. No more procrastinating. The children were in school, Daisy was stable for now, Andy was at work. If I could run today, the coldest and most miserable day of the month so far, I could run any day. So, I ran 5K, and I loved it. That old feeling came back as the endorphins flooded my body, my cheeks became rosy and I could feel some of the stress peeling away from my shoulders.

Soon, 5K became 10K and then I re-joined my old running club, the Wimbledon Windmilers. I had spent so long being someone's mum or Andy's wife that I had forgotten what it was to just be *me*. Running filled the gap that had opened up after I had so abruptly given up my career to become a full-time mum and carer. Buzzing with adrenaline and new ideas, thanks to running, I decided to enter races and use them as an opportunity to fundraise and raise awareness of our hospice.

It was seven years since we had first been accepted for care by Shooting Star Chase hospice and I decided to mark this by running seven races, a mixture of half-marathons and 10Ks, over the year, in order to raise sponsorship and awareness. The hospice continued to be a lifeline to our family during this time.

It seemed appropriate that the first race I took part in was the Atlantic College 10K on Mother's Day in 2012. Organised by my dad's old running club, it was wonderful to be back in Wales and running along the lanes around the school that had shaped me so profoundly.

Running became my outlet for dealing with the stress in my life. It brought me new friends and I soon discovered the joy of muddy puddles and blustery runs in Richmond Park. With a home life that revolved around the aseptic non-touch technique to prevent sepsis, hibiscrub and alcowipes, to be free to run in mud was life-affirming and liberating.

I was also aware that Xanthe needed time to be herself. It's tough when your brothers and sister and their additional needs take up so much of your parents' time. We did our best to make time for all four of our children and made sure they each had one-to-one time with us too.

Andy took Xanthe to her first Arsenal FC game, carefully explaining the offside rule to her and hoping she would love his club as much as he did. I'm not sure if she shares his love of football but all of our children know when asked who they support to answer: 'Arsenal'.

Music was the biggest passion shared by us as a family. Andy and I had bonded over our mutual love of music when we first met, and later we shared playlists with Xanthe and the boys and encouraged all of the children to widen their musical tastes and listen to as many genres as possible. This may have meant having to go along to hear some obscure thrash metal band play at Brixton Academy on occasion, but at least the children had their own tastes and didn't follow the crowd. They were growing up with their own opinions and strong personalities.

When Xanthe was in her final year of primary school, and while Andy held the fort at home, I decided to take her to her first festival. So much of our time had revolved around hospital and the needs of the other three children that it was wonderful to get away just girls together and forget about everything else going on at home. Of course, it was Glastonbury Music Festival. Where better to start your festival career?

One of Andy's colleagues, knowing that we had previously owned a VW campervan, offered us his van on condition we restored it back to its former glory as it was currently unused and rusting in storage and he was leaving the country to work in the US. The van replaced the Harley-Davidson that Andy had ridden for many years.

Andy had loved his Harley but once he started working for himself and didn't need to commute into the city each day it had little use. Piling children and all of Daisy's medical kit onto a motorbike was, frankly, impractical.

Instead our Nimmo Fun Bus was used whenever possible. Andy took Jules and his friends for a bushcraft day in the woods where they made a fire and cooked. He even managed a couple of camping trips with the boys. Daisy loved riding in the van.

Most of all we loved to use our hospice respite nights to take the older three children away to a festival and just let our hair down. Here we could relax, surrounded by lovely people and music, and sleep under the stars, which was the Nimmo way of unwinding. None of us wanted to lie on a beach.

We made sure we celebrated milestones and anniversaries, aware that each one was precious and important for making memories. The children's birthdays always involved parties and gatherings of friends. Daisy's birthday, so close to Christmas, descended into a feast of presents, cake, balloons and complete over-indulgence as we made up for so many previous milestones spent in the care of the NHS.

2012 was a big year of celebrations and family fun. Looking back, it was a reasonably stable year for the whole family and gave us the best memories ever.

When Daisy was only a few months old, I had sat with her in my arms watching the TV when London was announced as the winning host for the 2012 Olympics. I didn't even know if she would be around in 2012 and yet here we were, seven years later, down that long road travelled and Daisy was still with us.

I have a photo taken at the Olympic rowing venue at Dorney Lake, Eton. We had places at the wheelchair viewing area close to the finish and were there when Team GB won its first gold in the London Olympics. It was a wonderful day on so many levels. The photo of our family with our Union Jack flags, relaxed and happy, is my favourite ever.

That September we celebrated our twentieth wedding anniversary, managing to get away for a few days on our own thanks to meticulous military planning on my part.

I cajoled Andy into a couple's photo shoot to mark twenty years of married life. We had married in the days before digital photos and our wedding photos can really only be described as '*of their time*'. Now at least we had some proper photos of the two of us together, happy, relaxed, the real Andy and Steph, despite everything that had happened. Andy was whispering inappropriate comments in my ear throughout the whole shoot and making me burst into fits of giggles.

Our special year was rounded off with Andy's fiftieth birthday at the end of November. Daisy was in Great Ormond Street, recovering from more surgery to her bladder and bowel. There was no let-up, but we knew that it was important to celebrate Andy's milestone, just as we had our fortieth birthdays. How serendipitous that decision turned out to be.

Andy's fiftieth was nearly a year in the planning. I embraced the project and he shrugged. *"Here we go, Steph's got another thing that's going to take over our lives,"* I could hear him thinking. It was a brilliant party as everyone who came still agrees. We paid for a private nurse to sit with Daisy on the ward overnight (there was no way I was going to postpone it just because she was in hospital).

Friends came from all over. We held the party in a pub close to central London. There was a band and dancing, a chill-out room, and Andy played DJ (with the teenagers taking over when he got distracted). Xanthe and Theo made speeches. It was wonderful. Despite getting back to our hotel at 2am, I was still back on the ward with Daisy by 8am, telling her all about Daddy's party.

Andy didn't worry about getting older. Fifty was the new forty, and despite everything we were having fun, making memories, living our lives. Yes, we had more than our fair share of complications but we were making the best of it, living for the moment, seizing opportunities when we could. We refused to be defined by what life had thrown at us, instead relishing the good times.

Then, the day after his fiftieth birthday, Andy tripped while running to catch a train and broke a bone in his hand. Six weeks in plaster, no driving, no lifting. It was the story of our lives! In fact, it's a carer's biggest fear, that something will happen to them that means they can't look after their loved one. What happens to their dependent if a carer becomes incapacitated? We were lucky that there were two of us able to manage Daisy's complex care needs at that time, although it did mean that my workload doubled.

With an arm in plaster, Andy couldn't draw up IVs or change catheters or stoma bags, but at least he could still be around after work to read stories and supervise homework. It was just one of those things and with everything we had already faced, not the biggest of disasters, although one we could have done without.

CHAPTER FOURTEEN

"Explain to me again who you are dressed as?"
"We're Finn and Fionna from Adventure Time
Mum, have you actually even seen it?"

It was a sunny May bank holiday weekend. Andy and the older three children were off to their first-ever Comic Convention in East London. Cosplay was to become a huge part of Xanthe's life and Andy was not making any secret of the fact that he couldn't wait to immerse himself in the total geekery of a convention.

I was off to see my friend Jan and her friends play in a netball tournament, which was also a fundraiser for Shooting Star-Chase as one of their teammates had also received support from the hospice for her son.

It was a lovely day. Daisy enjoyed watching the netball and shopping at the little craft fair that was running alongside the tournament. I had a chance to catch up with friends, relax and chat in the warm, early summer sunshine.

Daisy was on good form, happy to see my friends and their children. She needed to use a wheelchair for much of the time but could still walk independently for short distances and she was determined to be in on the action with the other girls as they sat on the ground laughing and joking.

Watching her proudly I noticed she looked a little bit pale and the thought crossed my mind that she might be sickening for something.

We all arrived back home at the same time. Theo, Xanthe and Jules disappeared off to their rooms to inspect all their purchases from the convention and post their pictures on social media. Andy was beginning to prepare dinner in the kitchen.

He was a brilliant cook and had taken over preparing most of the family meals. I cooked well once upon a time but the demands of my family left me resorting to pizza, pasta and baked potatoes whereas Andy would spend hours creatively putting together some recipe he had seen on the internet.

Thanks to a grant from our local authority we were, at long last, having the house adapted to support Daisy's increasing physical limitations. She would always be small for her age, tests had shown that she had insufficient growth hormone. Her heart condition meant that she could not cope with too much exercise and would tire easily, stairs were becoming a problem and her visual impairment meant that they were also a risk.

As Daisy was growing up it was evident that we would need to make adjustments and changes to our home to accommodate her increasing needs. I couldn't carry her safely upstairs anymore and we needed to think about bathing and washing her as she grew bigger. Her bedroom was having a wet room added and a new stair lift was also on order. While this was going on, Daisy's bedroom had been moved to the front room and we had all de-camped to the back of the house.

Daisy was still able to walk fairly independently at that point and as she pottered around her temporary bedroom looking for a book I started preparing her bed and medication ready for the evening routine.

The next minute she let out a blood-curdling scream I will never forget because I have never heard anything like it before or since. She collapsed to the ground white as a sheet and went rigid. I screamed for Andy. There was something clearly very, very wrong, I thought she was having a heart attack. Catastrophic cardiac events are not uncommon in Costello syndrome and we knew of other children and young people who had suddenly dropped dead from one.

Andy ran into the room and picked Daisy up. As soon as he did she began to convulse violently in his arms, turning blue. I called 999, thinking this was it. We were losing her.

This turned out to be Daisy's first epileptic seizure. Despite everything that preceded it, this was one of the most harrowing things I have witnessed. Daisy was blue-lighted to A&E, unconscious and on oxygen. She was taken into resus and stabilised. Once she was conscious again there seemed no point in keeping her in the hospital, so we brought her home, worried about this new turn of events. Was this a one-off seizure? Was it the sign of something sinister going on–did she have a brain tumour or a bleed?

Over the following weeks the seizures escalated. A CT scan did not show any obvious malformations, but the neurology team at Great Ormond Street were contacted for advice. Daisy was started on intravenous anti-epilepsy medication and we were provided with 'rescue medication'—pre-filled syringes of midazolam, a powerful sedative to be used if she had prolonged seizures—and we began to keep charts documenting the type, time and duration of each seizure.

The seizures would knock her for six and she would become very disorientated and anxious afterwards, not knowing when another seizure was about to strike.

There were many blue light trips that year as Daisy's seizures proved difficult to control. We began to learn yet another new language, the language of epilepsy. Scans and extended EEGs showed that there were no 'put right-able' reasons for Daisy suddenly developing such severe and uncontrolled seizures; it just was another piece of her puzzle that did not add up. We knew that the seizures were multi-focal, firing from different parts of her brain. Why they had started, no one could tell us.

The worst thing about the epilepsy, apart from the unpredictability of the seizures, was that either they, or the meds she was on to try and control them, took away a little bit of who she was.

Like an unwelcome house guest, epilepsy took away a huge part of Daisy's life as she lurched from one seizure to another. It took us away from the other children as we stayed glued to her side to make sure she was safe. It carved up our family so that we constantly listened out for that first cry and the call from the person with her. It was a brooding presence when we left the house, determined that life should go on but secretly dreading the moment she had a seizure in a public place.

Jules, with his extreme anxiety, found it very hard. During the countless times he was sitting next to Daisy in the car as she would suddenly have a seizure, his expression was one of terror. All the children hated going out with her, not knowing if she would have a seizure and plans would have to rapidly change.

The seizures brought a deterioration in Daisy's physical abilities, whereas she was once able to stand and walk for short distances unaided she began to rely more and more on her wheelchair. She could no longer focus on activities for an extended time, flitting between her toys and books, unable to settle.

Her behaviour became more challenging and she started to hit out, her speech deteriorated, she developed echolalia, a pattern of repeating sentences and questions over and over as a way of coping with anxiety. It felt as if all her development had been put on hold, like a lift stuck between floors. I felt that epilepsy had stolen a little bit of our girl.

Epilepsy really turned our world upside down more than anything that had come before. We lived our lives on a knife edge now, not knowing what each day would bring, Andy and I agreed that we could take TPN and bladder issues, the surgeries and everything else that was involved in looking after Daisy, but seizures were the cruellest joke. We would be lulled into a false sense of security, a few weeks with maybe just a few minor seizures and some daily absence seizures (the irony) and then bang! The tonic-clonics would be back with a vengeance.

An international Costello syndrome family conference was planned for that summer, just like the one we had attended many years ago, before Daisy had become so incredibly complex. This time instead of Portland, Oregon, the conference was to be held in Florida and we decided to try to get there.

Andy had asked for donations towards the cost of the trip for his fiftieth birthday and we had the support of a local charity who were helping with the enormous costs of travelling to the United States with Daisy and all the medical equipment she needed.

We had always felt able to brave a return trip to the United States until epilepsy arrived. Now there was no way we could risk a transatlantic flight with Daisy's seizures being uncontrolled. She needed too many emergency hospital visits; there was no way she would be allowed onto a plane and there was no way we could safely care for her so far away from home. In the blink of an eye, Daisy's world, and ours, shrunk.

Life was just getting more and more complicated. We had to trade in our lovely car with its fabulous music system for a wheelchair-adapted van as we could no longer lift Daisy into and out of the car seat. The home adaptations finished, she was moved back into her bedroom. We now had a lift and hoists plus an indoor wheelchair.

Friends we had made in the Costello syndrome community were seeing their children developing and growing out of their medical problems, yet we were seeing Daisy regress. She was now on TPN twenty-four hours a day and with numerous intravenous infusions morning and evening to manage her seizures, infections and pain.

On top of that, we worried about our boys. Theo had started an apprenticeship in Information Technology, working and studying at a local college. On the surface he seemed to be doing okay but we didn't dare take our eye off the ball.

Jules was refusing to go to school and I was battling with our local authority to put in place the plans and funding he needed to attend a specialist school. But we were hitting a brick wall and so had no choice but to start tribunal proceedings.

At this stage I felt like everything was conspiring against us. We were being knocked back again and again, but were as determined as ever to get back up and keep moving forward, to ensure our children's futures. They deserved to have the childhood and education they needed.

Andy and I made a great team. If I found I was banging my head against the brick wall with yet another local bureaucrat, Andy would move his own appointments and come along to the meetings. His coaching skills were invaluable and we were always able to get the outcome we had aimed for—without burning bridges.

We had learned early on that the world of special needs was a small one, that the same faces and names cropped up again and again, and that the reputation of families went before them in the panels and meetings that took place to decide a child's fate.

We were determined to get what our children needed but in a way that was business-like and realistic, and we gave praise and thanks where it was due. Other people complained in hospital but our attitude had always been: *what can we do to make this better?*

As a result, despite our limited time, we gave what spare time we did have to fundraise, share our story or become involved as parent representatives or volunteers. Despite the battles with bureaucracy we were aware how lucky we were to live in a nice suburb of London, in our own home with one of the best children's hospitals in the world on our doorstep. We took nothing for granted.

We assimilated each problem and issue thrown at us and made things work. We were determined to remain optimistic and realistic. Andy was more the realist. Sometimes I was a bit too Pollyanna-ish in my overwhelming optimism and desire to enjoy family activities and time together. I planned events and days out and if they happened, they happened, but if they didn't then we would move on towards the next plan. Thinking back, maybe I could have just chilled out a bit more but I am so glad now that we fitted in so much.

Andy's business was going from strength to strength. He had a strong reputation in the recruitment sector as a coach and management development specialist and all of his referrals came via word of mouth. He had no need of my marketing skills. His clients rapidly became friends and the normality his working life gave him also sustained him when things were tough at home.

I was going for more and more extreme running goals. Since going back to running I had notched up a slew of half marathons and 10K runs as well as three more marathons and I was now setting my sights on become an ultra-runner, running past the marathon distance, and maybe even in the long term branching into triathlons.

I would get up on a Sunday morning and pound the trails in nearby Richmond Park, clocking up the all-important miles I needed as part of my ultramarathon training, then returning home where Andy had held the fort, normally making homemade bread and something delicious for lunch.

Our circle of friends, and our wider network of special needs friends and support groups, kept us going and social media meant that, although we could no longer be spontaneous and meet up with old friends on a whim, we could at least meet up online and share our lives with them.

In 2008, determined to make sense of our lives, I started my blog. Daisy had just started on TPN and writing became my therapy, as I attempted to put into words the impact of parenting three children with diverse special needs (as well as their sibling) and all the challenges faced not just by our family, but by countless families like ours.

While I relaxed by pounding away on the keyboard or going on a long run, Andy enjoyed his work, the ever-changing fortunes of his beloved Arsenal Football Club and extended games of online poker.

At last we had regular respite. We were only able to use the hospice for twelve nights a year (their service is free and they receive no guaranteed government funding) but with nurses constantly in the house and Daisy's never-ending medical needs, we could never switch off while she was at home.

Hospice respite stays were the only way we could properly relax. We had been asking for a long time for a referral to a specialist respite centre for regular, guaranteed stays for Daisy but had always had our requests turned down on the grounds of cost. It took the seizures and deterioration in Daisy's health for us to secure our allocation of respite nights.

It was a tough call. Essentially we had to agree that for two nights a week someone else would be responsible for Daisy's care, but we were also aware that Daisy was continuing to defy the odds, despite her deteriorating health.

In addition our other children's needs were increasing as they reached their teenage years. We could not realistically be there for all of them, all of the time, while Andy was working this hard. We needed the guarantee of regular respite breaks where we knew Daisy was safe and we could focus on the rest of the family.

Andy began scheduling his business travelling to coincide with the respite nights so I would not be left alone caring for Daisy on her return. When he wasn't travelling, we could go out and watch a film or, as was mostly the case, collapse on the sofa in front of the TV together. I will always be eternally grateful to our social worker for pushing our case for respite. It turned out to be that special time so needed together as a couple and as a family.

I achieved a minor victory in 2013 when I persuaded Andy to come to Glastonbury. The Rolling Stones were headlining. Daisy was happily booked into respite at the hospice and I managed to convince Theo, Xanthe and Jules' schools that this was an educational opportunity for them not to be missed. We sat in the awning of our campervan with Andy's cousin Deb and her son, while Andy cooked breakfast and we cracked open a bottle of champagne.

"Cheers! No IVs to do tonight," I said as I raised my glass.

Despite all his reservations about mud, crowds and shared toilets, Andy loved every minute of it.

2014 rolled round and we were going to have to give Glasto a miss as Deb's sister, Issy, had announced her wedding for the same weekend. It was going to be a chance for all the family to get together, which was important given how rare such opportunities had become. Although we were disappointed not to get down to Somerset for our Worthy Farm fix, we made up for it by booking Latitude festival in Suffolk—and then we got busy planning our outfits for the wedding.

CHAPTER FIFTEEN

"It's going to be so great to get the family all together again, we must make sure we get plenty of pictures, these get-togethers are becoming few and far between."

Issy and Kev's wedding in the Hampshire countryside was a magical weekend. When you reach middle age the wedding invites start drying up. Family reunions tend to happen at funerals, with promises not to leave it so long next time.

Andy, always one to embrace a retail opportunity, had bought a new suit. Proud of his beautifully-groomed beard, he was a man in the full throes of a mid-life crisis, or as my teenagers described him: "*a hipster trying too hard*".

Daisy couldn't come to the wedding. The onset of seizures had taken its toll and her medical needs were becoming more and more consuming. She was booked into the hospice, leaving me to ponder how I could involve her in some way in this big family reunion. It seemed so sad that she would miss out on it all.

The children each had their own room at the hotel. Bitter experience had taught us that sharing was not an option. The boys needed a safe haven to retreat to when the noise and pressure of making conversation got too much, while for Xanthe it was space away from her brothers.

This was our life, a constant juggling of the needs of our family: our boys and their high-functioning autism, Daisy and the complexities of her disability, Xanthe and her need to have a break from being the only '*normal*' sibling.

Getting ready in our room before joining the wedding party downstairs, I thought Andy looked like a man who was enjoying too many of the finer things in life, a man carrying a bit too much weight. I was worried about this. There was a strong history of heart disease in his family.

When we met, I was vegetarian and persuaded him to come over to the '*dark side*' as his friends called it. Despite the jokes, he was strict about his vegetarian principles, never tempted when friends waved bacon butties under his nose. But Andy's business was going well, he was enjoying the fruits of his labours, lunches with clients, expensive Bourbon. I didn't want to lose him to a heart attack or for him to be reliant on medication to manage his blood pressure.

I made a mental note to do what I always kept promising to do, which was to plan healthier menus, shop for home-cooked meals, cut out the snacks. I needed my husband to be around.

Our children played with their cousins and I ignored the fact that one of my children was missing, another would not participate in the family photograph, preferring to stand to one side glaring at the camera while we all smiled, and another had disappeared off to bed halfway through the evening without saying goodnight to anyone. It was our norm. For a moment I envied the cousins with their children who sat engaged as their parents spoke, who played nicely, high academic achievers with glossy hair and bright smiles.

Andy and I had a family that stood out, but we were making it work. We were adept at sharing moments together and having fun. Moments like Issy and Kev's wedding, where our faces shone with happiness in the photos and we laughed as you can only laugh when family gets together and the wine flows.

A few weeks later we dropped Daisy off at the hospice for another respite stay then set off in the campervan to Suffolk for our weekend festival fix with Deb at Latitude.

We were celebrating Deb's fiftieth that weekend. Out of all his cousins he was closest to her in age and looked to her like a sister. We all shared a love of music and, drinking pints of cider, had a blast singing along to our favourite songs and trying to explain the slightly risqué cabaret to the children.

We had a very exciting appointment after we left the festival site, unwashed and tired. We were going to meet our new puppy, Pluto. The children and I had been persuading Andy that we should get a dog for almost a year.

I was worried that at seventeen, fifteen and nearly twelve, Theo, Xanthe and Jules were less interested in playing with Daisy these days; they had their own interests and circle of friends. Daisy's increasing disabilities meant getting out of the house and joining in activities with children her own age was becoming almost impossible. I had also done a lot of research around assistance dogs and thought that if we were to get the right breed, perhaps we could train the dog to support Daisy, or at least to warn us when she was having a seizure.

There was a lot of discussion about which breed of dog we should get. Andy was determined to win the argument and get a Husky. I, on the other hand, wanted a working Cocker Spaniel.

Obviously, I won and our beautiful, golden working Cocker Spaniel joined our family that September. We all met him when he was a tiny puppy, just after Latitude, as the breeder lived close by. They agreed to hold onto Pluto until he was a little older so they could work on his socialisation, and so that he could practice walking next to a wheelchair. The dog breeder's seven-year-old daughter had to sit, quite mortified, in her old all-terrain buggy while Pluto was taken out for walks on the lead so he would be used to Daisy's wheels when he arrived with us.

Andy and I drove back to Suffolk just before our wedding anniversary. Daisy was in respite and Andy and I were able to make the most of some precious time together too. We stayed in a beautiful old hotel and spent a wonderful, relaxing afternoon eating lobster and strolling by the sea, enjoying the last of the summer sun in Southwold before going to collect Pluto.

The children were thrilled when our puppy joined the family at last, not least Daisy, who had chosen his name. Pluto was her dog and he immediately bonded with her. Having a new puppy around felt like going back to the baby days but there was also the added bonus of walks with Andy in the local woods. My plan had worked. Not only did I want Pluto to be a companion and assistance dog for Daisy, but he would also force Andy to get out of the house and take more exercise to try and lose that middle-aged spread.

For the first few weeks of Pluto's arrival my plan went smoothly, then Andy started to get tired and grumpy. He was working too hard, about to start a big contract with a new client—this alongside family life, a new puppy and a wife who insisted on running crazy ultramarathons on a weekend. No wonder he had a short fuse. But he was pleased that the extra exercise from walking Pluto was paying off and he had to tighten his belt a couple of notches.

"Look at me, I'm losing weight, looking good," he said as he admired himself in the mirror.

He was always admiring himself. It was the actor in him: start with believing in yourself. In his eyes, he was an Adonis.

"How come? You're still eating the same," I replied, mainly wondering what his magic formula was when I was relying on running four times a week just so that I could still eat cake. Surely just taking the dog for a daily walk wasn't responsible for this sudden weight loss?

"Dunno, but don't knock it, I'm looking good."

I think the alarm bells rang. I like to think that they rang. For me that was the first moment of concern. Why had it not occurred to us that going down a belt size without trying at Andy's age was not a good thing? We were so caught up in keeping going, caring for Daisy, fighting for our boys, being there for Xanthe, running Andy's business, that something was bound to be overlooked.

And just like my dad before him, Andy put his tiredness down to getting older and our hectic lives, and I put his irritability down to just being a grumpy old man.

2014 was the year I was going to fulfil my dream of running an ultramarathon. I ran the London Marathon earlier that spring. I had one more late summer marathon, then I was going to test my mental strength by running 50K.

The race took place in early October and it was one of those races where everything came together as planned, not the fastest time, but a race where I felt good and in control and as if the months of training paid off. I broke it down into five 10K runs, each one ticked off as I moved closer to the goal of becoming an ultramarathoner. I had worked out my approximate finish time and Andy was going to meet me at the end, with the children and Pluto.

Everything was going to plan and as I entered the final 5K

of the race I kept myself focused by thinking about my family waiting at the finish line, Daisy cheering as she had so many times before, our over-excited puppy, the first time he had seen me in a race, Andy waiting proudly. They weren't there. For the first time ever, Andy had not made the finish line in time and it was to be a good half an hour before they arrived.

"I'm so sorry I'm late," he said. "I'm just feeling really knackered and getting them all into the car took such a lot of effort today. Honestly, it's like herding cats at times."

I did think at that point that I was asking too much of him. Training for these long runs, my Prozac as I called it, and expecting Andy to hold the fort while I was out, was unrealistic. I would have to slow down. Andy was tired. It was too much to ask. Just getting everyone into the car ready to come out is a military operation in our family. We were not getting any younger and life was not getting any easier.

By mid-October Andy began complaining of bad stomach pains and was experiencing some rectal bleeding. He went to our doctor immediately and was referred to a gastroenterologist for further investigations. He was feeling sicker and sicker and for the first time ever had to cancel his work commitments, having no energy to travel into London and work a full day.

We had a long-standing phrase in our family, 'Dr Theatre will get you through,' from his old days on the stage when the show had to go on. Dr Theatre had got him through on many a previous occasion but this time he really was too ill. I was worried.

Our doctor felt that, if anything, Andy was too poorly for it to be cancer. He was concerned that Andy had developed ulcerative colitis, an inflammation of the bowel. In many ways the symptoms did fit. Daisy had pancolitis (total inflammation of the intestinal tract) before she started on TPN and had experienced similar symptoms to Andy: rectal bleeding, pain, weight loss.

I Googled treatments and diets and steeled myself for the possibility that we would have two members of the family on special nutrition regimens and under long-term gastro-intestinal plans.

Andy went to the first appointment with the gastro consultant alone. I did not have any help for Daisy that day so I could not come along. I was surprised when he came home. I thought he had become so ill so quickly that the doctor would have arranged to admit him immediately. In hindsight I think Andy had been overly optimistic with the consultant during that first appointment, in denial about what was actually happening.

He was booked in for upper and lower endoscopies at the next available slot, the beginning of November. Those two weeks of waiting dragged as I watched Andy deteriorate before my eyes. He had no energy and could not eat. He was visibly gaunt and tired. He had lost around 20lbs in the space of a month. I was buying anything and everything I could to tempt him to eat and give him some energy.

The children just assumed that Dad had a stomach bug. I explained that the doctors were thinking he might have some sort of inflammation in his gut and that he might have to start a special diet. Daisy was too wrapped up in her new puppy to notice that Daddy was spending more time in bed.

Fortunately, the day of Andy's endoscopies coincided with one of Daisy's regular respite nights. I drove him to the hospital, relieved that at last we could get some answers and then focus on getting him better. Andy was feeling too ill to be worried anymore.

When the consultant came to see him prior to the procedure I told him exactly what was going on and how bad it was. He told me to wait, hopeful that they would find some answers once they put a camera into Andy's digestive system and had a good look. Andy was given some intravenous sedation to relax him for what is not the most comfortable of procedures. He looked tired and drawn.

We kissed each other and said goodbye as he was eventually wheeled off into the procedure room. I sat on the hard plastic chair in the brightly-lit ward and waited.

CHAPTER SIXTEEN

"Well, Andrew, I have found something and I'm sorry to say that it doesn't look good. It is highly likely that what I have found is cancer."

3rd November 2014

Andy just looked at me as the doctor continued speaking and mouthed the word, *"Fuck."*

Andy and I were sadly far too used to receiving bombshells, even ones as nuclear as this. We were shocked, but not really surprised. Andy had become so ill so quickly that there could be no other explanation. Of course it was cancer. Colorectal cancer.

The doctor started talking about how, if it had not spread, then survival rates were good. Cancer could be managed like a chronic disease. I remembered Dad, how he had died of the same disease almost exactly fourteen years ago. There were few treatments then. He had survived for only eight months from diagnosis. Andy, on the other hand, had so much more going for him. For a start, we had a private medical insurance policy.

Andy and I were so grateful to the NHS. We would always be the first to defend it. The NHS had saved Daisy's life on many occasions. It had saved my life when she had to be delivered prematurely.

But as the years ticked on, our children, Daisy especially, needed us to be fit and healthy so that we could support them. Andy's business had been going well and a few years previously I had taken out private medical insurance for both of us, justifying it on the basis that if we needed a minor surgery we couldn't wait or try and juggle respite dates with NHS availability.

I discovered the day Andy was diagnosed that our policy also included very extensive cancer cover. Cover that we were later to learn included treatments and therapies that were now no longer funded on the NHS as they were deemed too expensive, treatments and therapies that were clinically proven to extend survival time.

We went home, letting the news wash over us. How to tell the children? They had been through so much since Daisy was born and now they were going to have to cope with yet another, huge, life-changing bombshell.

When we left home earlier that day the children assumed that their dad had some sort of tummy problem and would probably need a specialist diet and drugs to sort it out.

We decided that they each needed to hear the news separately. Each child was different and had his or her own way of processing information. We agreed that we needed to be open and honest from day one, telling them what we knew, showing them that we were positive. Just as we always had been about Daisy. The important thing was to be truthful, but we didn't want to scare them. Nor did we want to give them false hope.

We didn't yet know what lay ahead, and as much as we were struggling with this news ourselves, it was going to be so much worse for our children, trying to assimilate and understand this next crisis. I longed to be able to protect them from it all, to keep it to ourselves and allow them to live their lives untroubled, but this was never our family way and they would soon smell a rat. We decided that Andy would tell Jules and Xanthe, and I would tell Theo.

I picked Theo up from the station on his way home from college, knowing that he would prefer a car conversation, where he didn't need to make eye contact.

Andy sat down quietly with Jules and Xanthe and broke the news to them.

Each of the children reacted differently. Theo went straight over to see his best friend Leo and tell him the news. Leo's mum very thoughtfully gave him a key to the house so that he could come over whenever he needed to.

Xanthe retreated to her room and her art, always the escape for her. We knew that her close friends would support her, which is exactly what they did.

Jules was not long past his twelfth birthday. It was over-whelming for him. For a few weeks afterwards he could not bear to be in the same room as Andy. He was struggling already, barely able to get through a day at school as we continued our battle to secure him a place in a residential specialist school. Now, unsurprisingly, he was scared that his dad was going to die. He was confused. It was all too much for a little boy, with so many issues of his own to process.

And then there was Daisy. We were so glad she was not in the house that night. We needed some time to absorb it ourselves and to be available for our older children.

The next day I contacted our hospice to tell them the news and to ask for advice on what to say to Daisy. I needed to respect the fact that she would see that things were different.

I didn't want to scare her, nor did I want her to think that whatever was happening with Andy was going to happen to her.

"Be honest, as you always are," advised the counsellor on the end of the phone.

Daisy was savvy enough to know things weren't right. So we told her Daddy had a poorly tummy and would need a '*wiggly*', a central line, just like her and that she would be able to tell him what it was like.

I mentioned the word cancer so that she would know that it referred to Daddy if she overheard other people talking about it. We told her that we loved her very much.

We were numb. But at least we had an answer to why Andy was so ill. Now the focus was on getting Andy better, on beating this cancer.

In so many ways life with Daisy had prepared us well. We were used to hospitals and the '*system*'. We knew how to discuss things like portacaths in preference to Hickman lines and if Andy needed a stoma bag, well, that was no big deal. We had been living with stomas and central lines and IVs for years.

The first stop was to stage the cancer, to determine how much cancer Andy had and where it was located. MRI and CT scans followed the week after the scopes. Then we were given the appointment to meet with the gastroenterologist to discuss the results.

Our hope had been that the cancer was contained within the bowel, that it could be operated on, maybe some chemo and radiotherapy, and then we'd take it from there. Sadly, it wasn't to be.

Cancer called the shots as it was to do so many times over the next year. It had already metastasised. It had spread from the primary site in Andy's bowel to his liver and there was also a suspicious spot showing up on his lung.

Andy's bloods showed he was clearly very unwell. He was anaemic, his liver function was poor and the tumour markers were high. I was used to seeing blood results, as I had to take Daisy's bloods on a regular basis to check how she was doing on TPN. I knew a bad set of results when I saw one.

It was amazing that Andy was still able to walk around and that he had, up to a few weeks previously, still been working and helping out with Daisy's care. He was very poorly.

I knew Andy needed to know all the facts so that he could plan how he was going to manage the situation. He did not want the doctor to hold back or sugarcoat anything. He did not want false hope, just facts. We asked the doctor to show us exactly what we were dealing with. He drew it out on a piece of paper.

First, he drew the liver, then he divided it up into the left and right lobe. He started drawing circles where the tumours were, one, two, three, four.

"You can stop now!" said Andy.

There were four large tumours crossing the two lobes. The cancer in its current state was inoperable. It was really about as bad as it could get.

When my dad had cancer, the focus had been to remove the primary tumour, the mothership. These days, treatments and surgical procedures had progressed hugely and the protocol for metastasised cancer like Andy's was to start chemo to shrink the tumours first. We met with Andy's oncologist to discuss the options and start to make plans.

We arrived at the cancer centre for our first meeting with Andy's oncologist, David, and the nurse specialist, Diane. It was at this point I realised that while I was still wrestling with the decision to go down the private medical insurance route it was absolutely the right one; Andy would start a protocol called FOLFOXFIRI.

It was a weapon of mass destruction and normally only reserved as a second or third line option, mainly for pancreatic cancer. Having medical insurance meant that Andy could miss out the cheaper *'let's give them a try and see if they work'* treatments and go straight in for the big guns.

Added to this would be Avastin, the wonder drug. It had just been taken off the cancer drugs fund list in the UK so would not have been available to him at that point if he were an NHS patient. Avastin is a very expensive monoclonal antibody, a form of immunotherapy treatment aimed at stimulating the body to mount a response against the cancer. It is clinically proven to extend life in advanced cancer.

CHAPTER SEVENTEEN

"What if this protocol doesn't work? Have we used up all our options by going straight for the big guns?"

All we wanted was options, a chance. Andy knew that being diagnosed with stage four metastasised colorectal cancer meant we could never use the word cure, but to manage it, to be cancer-free, that would be the aim. Whatever it took, he was prepared to try. "What if this protocol doesn't work? Have we used up all our options by going straight for the big guns?" Andy asked.

"Let's cross that bridge if and when we come to it," said David the oncologist. "There are always other options."

Andy's biggest priority in order to prepare himself for treatment was to understand the statistics. He played online poker to relax and knew that the cancer cards he had been dealt were not good, but he needed to work on his strategy for how to play them, and this meant knowing his odds.

I let the figures wash over me as David reeled off average survival rates. We knew from Daisy that that's all they were, figures and averages. There are so many other factors that came into play to ensure a good outcome and that's what Andy wanted to work on.

Andy had recently read an essay by the American evolutionary biologist Steven Jay Gould. Gould had been diagnosed with a very rare and aggressive cancer in 1982 yet he made a full recovery. *The Median Isn't The Message* discussed his reaction to the fact his cancer was incurable and would likely kill him within eight months and then his subsequent research that revealed the true significance of the term 'median survival rate'.

Gould's hypothesis was that if the median is the half way point it meant that for his cancer fifty percent of people would die within eight months of diagnosis. However the other fifty percent would live longer, potentially a lot longer. He identified the common characteristics of those in the favourable group and how he could use those to influence the survivability of his diagnosis.

Given that the cancer was detected early, he was young, optimistic and had the best treatments available he reasoned that he should be in the favourable half of the upper statistical range. After an experimental treatment of radiation, chemotherapy and surgery, Gould made a full recovery.

Andy needed to know what the median survival rate for his type and spread of cancer was, so he could ensure that the other factors which would determine his long-term survivability were in place.

He was very positive; he was educated, he had a close family and support network, he had access to great healthcare and the best treatments, he was relatively young and in good general health. His most important weapon against the cancer was his mind. Andy was an avid reader of military history and strategy and treated the cancer in the same way, arming himself with the facts about where it was and how it was to be treated in order to ensure he was in the best possible position for the treatment to work.

He needed to get his head in the right place and that meant working with Marion, the coach that he had trained with, the coaches' coach and the person whose skills he rated most highly. He worked with Marion to clarify his vision and goals for treatment, to revisit his hypnosis training and to visualise his cancer shrinking under the chemotherapy.

As an atheist Andy trusted the scientists, but as a neuro-linguistic programming practitioner, focusing on the impact of patterns of behaviour, he knew he could use his mind to influence the outcome. For him it was not a battle to be won or lost, it was about optimising his chances and identifying how best to play his cards.

Marion told me later he was very clear on his goals, to stay fit and strong, to be in a position to get back to work, to go to Glastonbury again. Andy did not fear death. He just had more living to do. She told me that it was only when they spoke about me and the children that he broke down. He could accept the fact his cancer was incurable and that he was going to die within the next few years, but he could not bear the thought of leaving his family behind.

It was too painful. We could not even go there as a couple and it remained an unspoken truth between us, too painful to contemplate.

Before chemo started we took a family photo, all six of us together (with Pluto), and individual shots of Andy with each of the children. I needed to have this last picture of us together before we entered a new phase in our lives.

Andy's first chemo was scheduled for his fifty-second birthday. There had been no time to fit a permanent central line so he opted to have the chemo through a peripheral cannula into a vein in his arm. This meant a slower infusion rate and an inpatient stay on the ward. He needed to get started; he was getting sicker by the day and if we didn't start treatment soon it would be too late.

The short-term goal was to reach the three-month treatment milestone. Chemo every other week, three days of infusions each time, then repeat scans. The hope would be that the tumours had shrunk and the inoperable liver tumours would now be operable. If that was the case, we told David, we had to go to Glastonbury. It was so important for us to recharge our batteries, to be away and just be us. We even dared hope that if things went to plan he could have the surgery done and dusted by the time we made our annual pilgrimage to the festival on Worthy Farm at the end of June.

Daisy taught us to have hope, and to have goals, short term, medium term, long term, but always be prepared to change the plan, as the goalposts moved. Our short-term goal was to spend Christmas together at home as a family.

CHAPTER EIGHTEEN

"Happy birthday Mr Nimmo, we hope you like chocolate cake."

I sat with Andy as he dozed, watching toxic liquid drip slowly into his vein. So far, so good. He was feeling well and we were happy and hopeful. There was a noise outside his room then all the nurses walked in with a big birthday cake and sang *'Happy Birthday'*.

"Surely this counts as the most surreal birthday experience yet," remarked Andy as he blew out the solitary candle.

Daisy found it hilarious that Daddy was now the patient, and the boot was on the other foot, but she seemed to take it in her stride. She held Andy's hand and her smile seemed to say, *"I know what it's like"*.

We reassured the older three that things were good, everyone was happy that treatment had started and now we could move on with dealing with the cancer.

A few days after chemo, Andy had a central line inserted under general anaesthetic. Now there were two people at home with central lines. When the doctor came to explain the procedure, he was taken aback when Andy reeled off the risks and the benefits.

"It's okay," I explained. "Our daughter is TPN dependent."

"I thought you were medical," he responded. "You sound like you should be."

"I'm as good as," I laughed.

Things were going well, too well. One evening, a few days after the chemo had finished and he'd had the surgery to insert his line, Andy started to feel ill, sweating, vomiting and constantly in the toilet with stomach cramps and diarrhoea.

I knew all about sepsis. I'd seen it before with Daisy. I thought I knew the signs. Sepsis in an adult can be insidiously different to sepsis in a child, however. I'd had years of watching Daisy, knowing the subtle signs. We were only one chemo in with Andy. How did we know that the incessant diarrhoea and vomiting were not down to the side effects of the toxic drugs he had just had pumped into his veins?

I called the ward for advice and while I was on the phone Andy weakly called out, "I think you need to call an ambulance." He was grey, shaking with rigors and had collapsed on the sofa. It was evident that he was gravely ill.

I had been through this with Daisy, the call to emergency services, reeling off her symptoms and diagnosis, the blue light trip to the hospital. Suddenly I was facing this situation with my husband. By some minor miracle Daisy was staying at our hospice for a respite break, otherwise I don't know what I would have done.

If it was scary for me and Andy, then it was ten times worse for the children who were hiding in their bedrooms, earphones on, distracting themselves with electronics, knowing that downstairs four paramedics were working on their dad.

"It's going to be okay," I shouted up to them. "But we need

to get Dad to hospital. We've been through this with Daisy so we know what we're doing. It's going to be alright."

I wasn't convinced. In the ambulance I looked at my husband, ashen, with an oxygen mask over his face and wondered if this was it, were we even going to make it to Christmas?

But he needed me to be strong. He needed to hear positive things, so I pulled myself together and grabbed his hand, looked into his eyes and said, "Andy, remember what you worked on with Marion? Remember your goals, your vision. Focus on them. I'll deal with the rest of the crap."

He was taken into resus and I phoned David. This was a new experience for me, not to be there in resus as I always was with Daisy, but this was adult services, this was another world. Andy had neutropenic sepsis. The chemo had wiped out his neutrophils, the infection-fighting blood cells, and he was susceptible to every little germ. His blood cells would need to recover to an acceptable level before he could have another round of chemo.

He was started on a series of injections to boost his neutrophils and just as with Daisy, we became obsessed with blood results. Blood count, liver function, inflammatory markers, this was already our language but now it also applied to Andy. And I kept my promise. He focused on keeping his mind in the right place, and I dealt with all the crap.

As a family we had always taken things one day at a time, and we continued to do this, while acknowledging that the children were obviously worried about things. All we could do was to encourage them to talk and share. We tried to lead by example, talking, sharing about how *we* felt. We had to live in the moment now more than ever, try not to mull and brood over what had been and what would be, just enjoy each day and appreciate the little things. Making pancakes, listening to music, reading aloud from a book. Being mindful.

When Andy was first diagnosed we also tried to lead by example with our friends and family. We needed them to know what worked for us as family and how to help. Our rules of engagement were simple and I posted them on my blog:

1. Be positive, no glum faces, no weeping and wailing.

2. Be practical. With a family as complicated as ours we need practical help. Our friends have been so generous in their time when we have had the inevitable crises that chemo and cancer bring; feeding the children, feeding us, walking the dog, offering lifts, just being there.

3. Little things mean a lot—knowing that people are thinking of us, even when they can't be here means so much—a text, a message, a card, an email. All these things have lifted our spirits to know that there is a lot of positive energy out there coming Andy's way.

4. This is going to be a long haul; Andy has been entered into the equivalent of the Marathon des Sables and the support crew is going to need to be there every step of the way.

A few weeks after the chemo had started, Andy's hair started to fall out. He was always so proud of his full head of hair, never losing an opportunity to compare it to his brother's balding pate. He got fed up of *"shedding like a Husky,"* so I took the clippers to his head and shaved it all off. The children were shocked at their dad's appearance but, as he said, it was about taking control and owning the cancer.

The list of stuff I had to deal with was huge: scheduling Andy's appointments, making sure he was eating good food, managing Daisy's care, ordering her medical supplies, trying to keep on top of her appointments, keeping an eye on what the children were doing at school, continuing our ongoing battle to get Jules into a specialist school for children with high-functioning autism, preparing for Christmas, planning for Daisy's tenth birthday.

Andy's blood count recovered well enough for him to have a second round of chemo before Christmas and another between Christmas and New Year. We celebrated Christmas with his cousin Deb and her son, Dominic, gathered around our table sharing food and stories, for once everyone co-operating and sharing in the moment. I treasure the picture I have of us all together; it was such a precious moment, for so many reasons.

We entered the new year with Andy attached to his home chemo pump. He was spending one night in hospital, then coming home for two nights attached to a pump. He would then spend a week or so in 'chemo fog' before emerging for a few days of normality before starting the next round of chemo. There was no way he could work.

He had last worked in October and even then it had been a struggle, but his clients were incredible.

"We're here when you're ready to come back," the messages said.

Andy had the most loyal client base a consultant could ever want. It meant the world to him.

CHAPTER NINETEEN

"I'm really craving Thai food today, let's go back to that little place in Merton Abbey Mills for lunch."

During the precious window of days when the chemo fog lifted and Andy became Andy again, we would seize the opportunity to have some normality back in our lives. Often Andy would be collected by a friend or work colleague and taken out for lunch. We would go and see a film or enjoy a meal out together.

These windows of wellness were so important that while many people wanted to see Andy and spend time with him, I sometimes felt resentful that they would steal him away, leaving me with him recovering from chemo, grouchy and short tempered with steroid rage.

I felt tired and emotionally drained, trying to keep up with Daisy's care as well as Andy's. I had not only lost another pair of hands, I had doubled my caring responsibilities and the person who would have normally supported me emotionally during this time was now the person being cared for. There were times during those months when I felt very lost and lonely.

But Andy needed to see people. He needed to be out and about to remind him that he was not just a patient and so I reluctantly shared him with his friends, knowing that it was an essential part of being able to keep body and soul together.

Conversely, I missed having time to myself. Prior to his diagnosis Andy was out and about every day, either working in his office or travelling to see clients. There was rarely a time that all four children were in school at the same time.

I couldn't even escape to my bedroom anymore. Andy was spending a huge amount of time in bed and when he was on his chemo pump it was difficult to share the same bed so I had taken up residence in the bottom bunk in Jules' room. I would often find myself awake at night, lying in the small bunk bed, wondering how my life had come to this.

I knew I needed to look after myself but my time was more limited than ever. I set the alarm for 5.30am twice a week and joined the early morning Dawn Raiders group in my running club so that I could get my running fix and time out for myself.

Our nursing homecare package was increased so that I wouldn't need to spend every evening setting up intravenous infusions when I needed to be cooking a healthy meal for Andy or attending an oncology appointment with him.

Daisy's needs were so great that she could only be looked after by an IV-trained, experienced nurse or Andy or myself. Andy had been unable to undertake any of Daisy's care since the end of October. Now, not only was I caring for someone with aggressive, stage four, incurable cancer, but I was also the sole carer of a TPN-dependent, highly complex little girl. This was without factoring in the needs of the rest of the family.

Sometimes the nurses were unavailable to cover a shift and, amazingly, Andy would find hidden strength so that I could leave him and focus on Daisy. The older children rallied around to get him endless glasses of the Italian lemonade with ice he craved. We were also receiving two nights a week funded respite for Daisy and we tried as much as possible to fit appointments and chemo around those days when Daisy was not in the house.

I liaised with Daisy's doctors to keep her outpatients appointments to a minimum but her own health was deteriorating and conversations were beginning to take place about yet another operation for her. Her bladder was failing and she was in increasing pain.

I left it to the doctors and surgeons to decide whether the risks of putting her through an eight-hour surgery to enlarge her bladder and deal with some intestinal issues outweighed the benefits. I had too many decisions to deal with. We would cross this bridge when we came to it.

Jules was still refusing to go to school. His entire life had involved watching his little sister become more and more medically complex and now his dad had cancer. No wonder he wouldn't go to school. He was receiving support from children's mental health services, but was clearly very stressed and we had hit crunch point.

"I have to get my son into a safe place before his dad dies."

This was the ultimatum I gave our local education authority. I was not over-dramatising the situation. I needed to know that Jules was in a school where he could feel secure and happy, where he would have the psychological support needed to deal with the forthcoming grief and anxiety. He needed a safe space just to be the little boy he was.

It took an intervention from our Member of Parliament, several meetings, multiple letters, emails and phone calls, the commencement of tribunal proceedings and ultimately Jules' being excluded from school because of his stress and anxiety for our local authority to agree to fund his place at a smaller, specialist school.

All this time spent in bureaucratic wrangling and red tape should have been spent with Andy and the rest of the family.

By Easter we achieved our goal and Jules had started at his new school. For the time being he was safe and in a place where his needs were understood. I mentally ticked that issue off my list.

Xanthe was in her GCSE year, trying to remain focused on her studies, trying to stay positive. Theo was finding the rigours of his apprenticeship difficult to cope with without the support he was used to receiving in school.

Daisy's nursing care would sometimes break down leaving me to do a waking night shift then focus on Andy's needs during the day. There was little time for me but I knew that I had to get through and look after myself if we were to have a chance of being a family and enjoy some sort of quality of life.

Running, of course, was important, but so was meeting friends for coffee or a few hours away from the house while Andy was having chemo and Daisy was in respite.

But my little windows of respite and time for myself were becoming smaller and smaller. Cancer and chemo had become part of our lives, just as so many other things had before.

When Andy was diagnosed, the doctor turned to me and said, "This will bring you to your knees."

I looked at him and thought, '*It will take more than this to break us.*'

He had no idea of the storms we had already weathered.

Our resilience strengthened with every knock and every setback. We were stronger people because of what we had been through with Daisy. This was our biggest-ever test but we had been in training for it for years.

CHAPTER TWENTY

"Is there anything you really, really want to do before you die?"

I asked Andy one day, early on in his treatment, what he wanted to do before he died. "You know, a bucket list. Obviously getting your pilot's licence or becoming a striker for Arsenal might be a bit much to fit in around chemo, but is there anything you would like?"

"I have done everything I have ever wanted, I have seen everything I have wanted," Andy said. "Of course, the list is endless but in a lifetime you are never going to do it all. Yes, there are more places I would love to go, things I would like to do but I have no regrets. My life has been so full." Then he smiled. "But maybe there are a couple of things I'd love to do before I die."

"Name them," I said.

"I want to meet Dave Grohl and I want to see Arsenal play in the FA Cup final."

So, I got to work. One wish was marginally easier to facilitate than the other.

By April, Andy had been given nine rounds of chemo, a total of twenty-seven days with toxic chemicals dripping into his bloodstream day and night. A scan after round six of the chemo had shown that the tumours had shrunk by fifty percent but it was not all good news.

The tumours on Andy's liver were still inoperable. The problem wasn't the size of the them, it was where they were—pressed up against major blood vessels, putting surgery out of the question. So, the plan was to tweak the chemo, swap one of the monoclonal antibodies for another that could target the gene mutation in Andy's tumours and see if that did the trick to shrink the awkward tumour away from the blood vessels and make it operable.

Andy was already struggling with some of the side effects of long-term chemo. He was losing sensation in his feet and started using a stick to walk. His sense of taste had altered completely and he could no longer enjoy the red wine we loved so much. One of the new drugs caused really bad skin rashes, but he was prepared to put up with all of these side effects in the knowledge that hopefully they were doing the trick and shrinking the tumour.

He was so positive and focused. Yes, cancer had made things a bit more complicated than we had initially thought but there were still options, there was a plan, there was hope and his head was in the right place.

His Facebook update said it all:

'What is good is that out of it I've become really clear about how I've made this work. It's about having a positive and realistic outlook with the ability to see different perspectives.

It is about living my beliefs, my values and using the innate things that are inside all of us and applying them to work towards the goal.

It's five months since diagnosis and the majority of that spent feeling fatigued and sick, but without Steph this positive state and confidence would not have happened, as much as I can look after myself mentally, she has been the driver of everything to enable me to do this and to brilliantly deal with our already 'complicated' life. I am beyond grateful for that and to you my friends who have been there with me in so many ways, including the lunches!

So, happy days, as I have choices and that's what it's all about, being able to choose to live the way you want and to drive forward whatever you think is in your way.

Onwards and upwards.'

Five months in, there was still a lot that needed to happen before the tumours could potentially become operable, but we were both positive, focused, and Team Nimmo was doing what it did best, thriving, not just surviving.

I decided to see what I could do to make Andy's bucket list wishes happen. Arsenal reaching the FA Cup final really was out of my hands but I could try my darndest to get a meet and greet with Dave Grohl, the lead singer of the Foo Fighters.

Twenty years previously, in the days before children, while Andy was still a professional actor, he had a summer season job in repertory theatre in the Lake District. I would go and visit him every few weeks and between those times he would spend the long evenings after shows listening to the radio – there was no internet in those days and the Lake District was a world away from twenty-four-hour party scene London.

On one of my visits he played a CD by a new band he had really got into that summer. Dave Grohl, the former drummer of Nirvana, had formed a band called the Foo Fighters. The following year Andy went along to their first UK gig at King's College in London. From those early days the Foo Fighters were up there with the Clash as one of Andy's all-time favourite bands.

Their *Sonic Highways* album had been released around the time of Andy's cancer diagnosis and it became the soundtrack to his illness and treatments. For Andy, meeting Dave Grohl was not about granting a terminally ill man's dying wish, it was about shaking the hand of a man whose music had played such a huge part of his life for so many years.

I tweeted every contact I could possibly think of and asked people to share my request far and wide. The Foo Fighters were headlining Glastonbury. We had tickets. Now, did anyone know how we could make it happen for Andy to meet Dave?

It worked. His people got in touch. Dave had read my blog and had asked them to make it happen. We were jumping for joy. What an amazing boost. Not only were we going back to Glasto, we were going to meet Dave Grohl and watch the Foo Fighters play from the side of the Pyramid Stage.

"Unbefuckinglievable," Andy said. He was the happiest I had seen him in a long time.

But first we had another plan in mind. We had not been to Scotland together since I was pregnant with Daisy but careful juggling of respite and chemo days meant that we were able to fly up together to see his family and then spend a few days in Glasgow.

Each of these moments; visits to football matches, reconnecting with family and friends, plans and projects, they all gave Andy the fuel and energy he so needed to continue his relentless march onwards through chemo after chemo, weathering the side effects in the hope that the toxic chemicals were doing their job.

I was giving him daily injections of blood thinners alongside the ones to stimulate his white blood cells and prevent another episode of neutropenic sepsis. One of his scans had shown that he had a pulmonary embolism and so another problem was added to the list of problems to be dealt with. The injections stung, like an extended bee sting, and I hated doing them, but Andy knew that the alternative of sudden death from the embolism causing a fatal stroke was far worse. He got through by shouting out as many expletives as he could.

When I was away in hospital with Daisy and he had to inject himself he resorted to belting out Beethoven's *'Ode to Joy'* at the top of his voice to get through the injection pain. The irony. That was the music we had walked down the aisle to after we were married.

Then, good news! Arsenal reached the FA Cup final. We couldn't get tickets but Andy roused himself from his post chemo fog to watch the match at home and the Gunners did him proud. They brought home the FA Cup and Andy's cheers could be heard in the next street.

He felt so uplifted. Arsenal had won, we were off to Glasto and not only that, we would be meeting Dave Grohl and seeing the Foo Fighters. There were only a couple more chemos before he could have a few weeks' break, negotiated with the oncologist, in order to have as much energy as possible to go to Glastonbury. But first there was the scan.

We added a new word to our vocabulary, *'scanxiety'*: *Cancer sufferers' description of the fear and anxiety felt at the end of a course of chemo, when they hope that it has done its job.*

You hope that having more side effects is an indication the

chemo is working, but really there is nothing to reveal how well the chemo has worked. The only way of knowing is by scanning the area and then waiting for the report to be written and sent to the oncologist.

There was always a waiting game, always hoping. At least I could keep busy. Daisy demanded so much of my time that what little I had left was shared between the competing needs of the children and Andy.

However, Andy had a lot of time on his hands. Waiting between chemos, between scans. Waiting for appointments, results. He'd always had at least two books on the go for as long as I had known him, but the chemo affected his concentration and sometimes it was easier to switch on daytime TV and let it wash over him as he whiled away the hours.

CHAPTER TWENTY ONE

"Dave Grohl's fallen off stage and broken his leg."

Andy's chemo was scheduled for my birthday, so we had gone out the day before to see the Alexander McQueen exhibition at the Victoria and Albert Museum in West London and discovered the Chelsea Physic Garden afterwards, walking around and enjoying each other's company before getting back for the school run.

I had taken Andy to hospital for his chemo on my birthday morning, posting on Facebook that the best gift I had been given was to wake up next to him.

It was now chemo day three and he was at home on a mobile pump that slowly dripped the infusion into his blood stream day and night. In the bedroom upstairs Daisy's TPN was dripping into her bloodstream.

My phone pinged.

Dave Grohl's fallen off stage and broken his leg.

WTF!!! I checked Twitter. It was true.

Only a couple of songs in, Dave Grohl had fallen off stage during a Foo Fighter's gig in Sweden. Incredibly he returned to the stage after medical attention and finished the set in a chair, dosed up with painkillers and with a very badly broken leg being held in place by medics. So rock and roll. So like my husband's attitude. Dr Theatre got him through!

"Well, it is what it is," Andy said when the confirmation came that there was no way the Foo Fighters were going to be able to headline Glastonbury. "We almost got to make it happen but the most important thing is WE are going to Glastonbury, that's all that matters."

The following week Andy went back to the hospital for another MRI. I have only ever had one MRI scan in my life and it was terrifying. Andy, by now, had had dozens of MRI scans. Enclosed in the claustrophobic tunnel, trying to tune out the bangs and knocks of the scanner as the magnets and radiowaves built up a picture of his organs and the tumours that were growing on them.

The contrast dye that Andy was injected with to highlight his tumours made him dizzy and vomit; he had to lie still, often for an hour with only the soundtrack of power ballads played through the hospital-issue headphones for company, his mind trying to focus on staying calm in the coffin-like space, breathing through his anxiety, trying to manage his thoughts, not just about the scan but also what it might or might not show.

It wasn't good news, but it wasn't all bad news. The extra rounds of chemotherapy that the oncologist and surgeons had hoped would shrink the tumours away from the blood vessels in Andy's liver had not made any difference. The good news was there was no new growth. The main tumour had shrunk considerably. It was fifty percent smaller than when Andy was diagnosed and the liver metastases had all reduced by between thirty to forty percent since diagnosis. It was never about the volume of cancer.

Andy had a lot of cancer and it was very aggressive, yes, but it was being kept at bay, it was just one very awkward tumour on his liver, probably no bigger than a coin, that was making surgery impossible.

David, Andy's oncologist, was, as ever, very optimistic. He always had a plan for something else to try and there were always options.

"I'm going to speak to the surgical team about radiotherapy," he said. "There's lots of exciting stuff happening in that field."

"Like cyberknife?" asked Andy.

He loved to hear about the technology and the science. We were so mindful that our private medical insurance meant that all the options were available to him so he wanted to know everything.

"There's a new treatment we are seeing some success with. It's called SIRT," David said. "I'm going to chat with my colleagues and see if this would be a suitable route for us to explore so we can progress to the surgery route."

SIRT, Selective Internal Radiation Therapy, was a relatively new treatment, which targeted liver cancers with tiny radioactive microspheres.

We left the appointment with renewed hope. Yes, the tumours had not shrunk, but they had not grown and there was a plan. That's all we wanted, a plan.

We returned home and focused on our preparations for Glastonbury. Andy was going to have an extra week off chemo so that his energy levels would be at their best and post-chemo side effects would not be a problem. As he was now registered disabled (the chemo drugs had severely affected his ability to walk and he was immunocompromised), he was eligible to use the accessible campsite and viewing platforms and to bring along a personal assistant to support him at the festival.

"I don't want you to be my helper at Glasto," Andy said. "You need a break from all the caring and worrying. I've got someone else in mind."

And that's how Keith, one of Andy's ex-colleagues, came to be part of our Glasto group. Part twenty-four-hour party animal, part carer, he was the perfect support, enabling Andy to get the most out of the festival without overdoing it.

I put together a spreadsheet of Andy's meds and injections and packed all his pills into labelled boxes together with a file of emergency information for us to take along, just in case. Andy added Keith to our campervan insurance and they were there as soon as the festival gates opened to bag a good spot and set up camp. Andy was buzzing. He didn't care who was playing. He was going to have a ball and forget about cancer.

Daisy was just as excited about going off to the hospice for her sleepover. Once she was happily settled and I had left instructions for the boys who were staying at home with Grandma, I went to pick up Xanthe and her friend from the school leavers' barbeque.

It had seemed a lifetime ago that she had started at high school, in her oversized blazer and kilt, excited to have left primary school and full of hope for everything her new school had in store.

Xanthe was blossoming into a beautiful young woman who knew her own mind. She had weathered so many storms over the years, being a sibling to a complex sister was tough enough, then to have the double whammy of her two brothers and their sometimes-annoying pedantry and habits. And now this year, her final year at the school, the most crucial year when she would sit her GCSEs, her dad had been diagnosed with cancer. Yet she remained as focused and determined as ever.

Xanthe was presented with the school cup for Bravery and Hope that afternoon. I was so proud I thought I would burst. I texted Andy a photo of Xan with her cup, engraved with her name. Bravery and Hope-qualities she had in bucket loads.

Xanthe and I joined Andy at Glasto later that evening. He and Keith had already set up camp and Deb had arrived. We fired up our barbeque and as we studied the programme, working out which bands we wanted to see and where there were clashes, Andy's phone rang. It was David.

I watched Andy as he paced up and down by our campervan, nodding his head, taking in whatever David was telling him.

"Please let it be good news," I thought. *"Please don't let anything spoil these next few days."*

We were in luck.

"They are going to try SIRT," Andy beamed. "Time to get blasted with those radioactive microspheres."

We hugged each other. We had a new plan. We were going to get those darned tumours operable and get our lives back. But first there was a festival to enjoy.

And enjoy it we did, every crazy, beautiful moment of our time at Worthy Farm. Andy was buzzing, his energy levels were really good and with Keith to support him, he got to do everything from party under the spider at Arcadia at midnight to witnessing the surreal moment when Patti Smith sang *'Happy Birthday'* to the Dalai Lama on the Pyramid Stage.

"Nothing I've not already said," he turned to me as the Dalai Lama spoke to the audience and gave his message of happiness and friendship.

As The Who played their last notes and the festival drew to a close we vowed to be back the following year. It was the goal to aim for, something to focus on to get through the next few months.

We packed up our campervan and headed back to London, batteries fully recharged. The weekend of music and laughter was the tonic we both needed to get ready for the next phase of treatment.

"Time to get radioactive," said Andy as we left the festival site. "I wonder if my pee will glow in the dark?"

CHAPTER TWENTY TWO

"The good thing about not having surgery in the next few weeks is that you will be able to go to Seattle."

The Costello syndrome conference was due to take place in late July and I was invited to present to medics during the event. I yearned to get back to Seattle where I had so many happy memories, from my student days researching my dissertation, to our wonderful, once-in-a-lifetime family road trip to the Pacific Northwest for the 2007 Costello syndrome conference in Portland.

I had wanted to go so much but had put it to the back of my mind. I did not want to leave Andy and anyway we were broke; there was no way we could afford the flights.

"It's meant to be. Daisy's booked into the hospice that week anyway, I've got chemo so we can't go away." Andy was insistent. "You need to go for both of us, and I think you should ask for people to help you get there."

I hated asking for anything. It felt like an admission of defeat. In the early days with Daisy it had been tough to ask for help, to accept help, but it had soon dawned on us that this wasn't an average parenting role we were undertaking and without support we would not be able to keep going. But asking for help to go to the Costello conference was in another league.

But I really wanted to go, not just because it would give me a chance to see our friends and meet with the medics to see if they could shine any light on Daisy's deterioration, but I had been asked to present at an information session during the medical symposium for the professionals at the forefront of research into Costello and related syndromes. What a fantastic opportunity to share Daisy's story with the people who were working on treatments and ways to manage the impact of the gene mutation that caused Costello syndrome.

"Seize the moment," said Andy. "That's our family motto, isn't it?"

So, I set up a crowd-funding page and within a matter of days had reached my target. I just needed help with the flights. It was high season and we had taken a big financial hit when Andy had to give up work following his diagnosis. I was still insistent that we could manage the hotel and other expenses involved.

Andy was feeling strong and positive. He would have the first round of tests to prepare for the SIRT treatment while I was away and if all went to plan then he would have SIRT when I returned.

I was worried about not being there for him. I had been there for all the scans and tests so far. He handed blood result print outs to me to interpret, I got him his favourite drinks and food and made sure he took his meds on time. But maybe I needed to go away? Maybe we both needed some space?

Being a carer is tough and caring for your partner is really tough. At least with Daisy we could make joint decisions, talk things through, share the caring. It was the same with caring for the boys, but now Andy was the cared for one and I felt incredibly isolated. There were times when he just needed to hunker down and focus on himself. He had to be selfish to survive but it left me to hold everything and everyone together.

Andy was right, just as he was right about bringing Keith to Glastonbury so that I could get a break. It was important for me to go away to Seattle to attend the conference and trust that our friends, all chomping at the bit, waiting to be asked, would help out. I booked the flights and confirmed to the conference organisers that I could both attend and present.

Andy was booked for an inpatient stay at the specialist liver centre where the SIRT would take place while I was away. The plan was for a trial run of the procedure using a dye instead of the radioactive microspheres to confirm that he was a suitable candidate for the treatment and plan for any potential issues. Having passed this stage, the microspheres would be ordered and he would be booked in for the full procedure on my return.

Everything was organised. Keith would take Andy to the hospital, Daisy was booked into respite, friends were organised to take care of our older children and the dog. I had no excuse. I packed my bag, hugged my family goodbye and boarded my flight.

Seattle was experiencing a heatwave. It felt so liberating to sit out by the hotel pool soaking up the sun's rays. Now able to be still, I absorbed the full impact of what I had been through over the past few months. I had been running on adrenaline, jumping around from crisis to crisis, keeping all our plates spinning, trying to be there for everyone. It felt good to stop, even for a second.

My Costello syndrome family welcomed me with open arms and I felt enveloped in their love. They had all been following our story on social media and through the blog. Many of the families had met Andy and it felt like coming home to a huge family reunion.

Again though, just as at the previous conference, I was left wondering why Daisy was so different to the other children with the same gene mutation. Yes, they all looked the same, with their curly hair, short stature, engaging smiles and fine-tuned sense of humour. But the children we met in Portland had gained skills, not lost them. Many could now read, speak. I only counted one other who was wheelchair dependent. No one was on TPN, no one had drug resistant epilepsy.

I met with some of the geneticists at the forefront of research into Costello syndrome. "It's highly likely she has some secondary syndrome going on but we just haven't discovered it yet," they said.

The other theory was that maybe there had been other children with Costello syndrome and the severity of Daisy's presentation but they had not survived. It was an accident of birth that Daisy was born into a comfortably well-off, middle-class family in a London suburb with one of the best children's hospitals on her doorstep. Maybe Stephen Jay Gould's essay about cancer and influencing outcomes applied to Daisy as well? With all the external factors in play—where she lived, access to healthcare, a supportive family—she defied the odds of the most extreme manifestation of her syndrome.

Much of what I could share about Daisy's case history helped to challenge the medics' assumptions about the syndrome and, as at the previous conference, I was able to pick up some useful information on the latest findings from the research community which might help the team back home.

A paper had just been published confirming the link between

Costello syndrome and autism spectrum disorder. I had long suspected that Daisy had autistic traits but now I had the documentary evidence: the need for predictable routines, anxiety, the constant repetition of words, which is known as echolalia, as a means of managing stress. I had seen some of Daisy's traits in the boys, so an autism diagnosis came as no surprise.

Once the conference had ended I had some down time for a couple of days. Time to catch up with a couple of Atlantic College friends who lived nearby, to take a bike tour of the area, to dream about coming back with Andy and touring the islands off the mainland, staying in a cabin, away from everything.

I sat in Pike Place market and called him. The pre-SIRT tests had gone well and Andy had been told he was an excellent candidate for treatment. Everyone was positive, we were moving forward. There was a plan.

"We'll come back here, to the Pacific Northwest, when you've had the liver surgery," I told him. "We'll make things happen to come back here and back to Canada too."

"I'd love that," he replied. He was still in his hospital gown, recovering from the procedure earlier that day, the steroid-induced insomnia making him restless. "Just you and me, cycling and hiking, cooking fresh fish on the barbeque and enjoying life. And of course, you know what else you can do in Washington State?"

"Buy cannabis legally?"

Since his diagnosis, Andy had researched the medicinal effects of cannabis on cancer pain. Not necessarily on its ability to shrink tumours—he put his faith 100 percent into the clinically proven treatments available for that—but as a way of reducing dependence on opiates and anti-nausea drugs. He was increasingly frustrated by the heavy-handed laws in the UK that criminalised cannabis use, meaning that he could be prosecuted if he was caught using cannabis to manage his cancer symptoms.

There had been so many occasions when we wished we lived in Holland or in one of the US states where cannabis was legal so he could use the oil to help manage all the side effects of both the cancer and the chemotherapy. We didn't need another incentive to get back to Seattle, but that was a useful one to have in the back pocket for when Andy was stable enough to travel.

I guess absence really does make the heart grow fonder. It was lovely to go away and spend a few days just being me, but it was even nicer to come home to my family, all back together under one roof again. We had all benefitted from the break and the house felt more relaxed and calmer than before I had left.

Andy's SIRT treatment was scheduled for the following week. He would be in hospital for two nights and the instruction sheet he was given stated he could not travel on public transport or sit too closely to anyone for an extended period, as he would be emitting radiation for a few days after the microspheres were inserted into his tumours.

As always, Andy devoured all the information he could about this new, revolutionary treatment—it was the stuff of science fiction. Tiny microspheres containing radioactive yttrium-90 lodge in the tumour, maximising tumourcidal effects and minimising healthy liver tissue damage.

"How lucky am I to have this as an option?" he said.

We knew that our private healthcare policy had made this possible, that we would have had to fight a huge battle if he did not have this cover. It was not just about the treatment, it was about minimising the stress and making sure everything happened quickly and efficiently, with joined-up communication.

We loved the NHS and always would, but our experience with Daisy had taught us that, when it came to keeping Andy alive and well, good communication between his teams was absolutely of the essence.

Andy spent most of the day of his treatment in the interventional radiology suite. Once he returned to the main ward he was very groggy and in quite a lot of pain. We were so positive, though, now that the treatment was underway and hopefully shrinking the tumours so that the diseased part of his liver could be removed and he could hopefully enjoy some stability.

The surgeons and doctors who came to review him felt the same. They were very excited about SIRT and had seen good results so far. We started mentally working out the possibilities.

It would be two weeks before the first scans but the main results would be visible a month after treatment. Hopefully, if all was good, that would mean that the liver surgeons could get in and operate a few weeks later and maybe, if Andy was strong enough, the primary tumour could be removed at the same time. With a good wind behind us, maybe by Christmas, the surgery could be behind him and he would be looking at a period of maintenance chemo. At least until the cancer returned. Whatever happened, the cancer would return.

Once it had spread to the liver and metastasised there was no way every single tiny little cancer cell could be mopped up by treatment. No one ever talked of curing Andy, just expressed the hope that it could be managed like a chronic disease.

"I need to focus on my fitness then, so I can be in the best possible shape for surgery."

"Once you get over the side effects of the SIRT," I reminded him. "Remember they said that you will feel really fatigued afterwards."

Andy commented on his Facebook a couple of weeks later how much he had underestimated the fatigue that would follow the SIRT treatment. It was bone-achingly debilitating.

We went on holiday to the Suffolk coast with Jules and Pluto. Andy made himself get up each day and join us for lunch or to sit in a chair on the beach but the effort would take its toll and he spent much of the time back at the cottage reading and snoozing. At least it was a change of scenery and that, coupled with a few bottles of the local brew, lifted his spirits. I hoped it would speed up his recovery.

CHAPTER TWENTY THREE

"The Foos have announced a gig in Milton Keynes. We have to go, it's just before our wedding anniversary too!"

Late that summer, not long after we came back from Suffolk, the unbelievable happened. The Foo Fighters announced a series of UK gigs. While recovering from his surgery and allegedly off his head on all the painkillers, Dave Grohl had drawn a picture of a throne with guitars and lasers that he could sit on during shows so that the band could continue their tour. And in true Foo Fighters style it happened. They were coming to the UK to play.

And that is why, on an unseasonably cold Sunday evening at the beginning of September 2015, Andy and I found ourselves at the side of the stage while the greatest rock band in the world played.

Andy, dosed up on painkillers and steroids, was high on the adrenaline of excitement and his face said it all. There had really only been one thing he wanted to do before he died and that was to shake the hand of the man whose music he loved so much, the music that from the Nirvana days until now was the soundtrack to our lives.

Afterwards, we sat in the backstage bar waiting for the crowds to go and scrolling through the pictures on our phones, when I looked up to see a tall, grinning man on crutches stood next to us.

"Hey man," said Dave Grohl, as he tapped Andy's leg with one of his crutches. "Are you gonna talk to me or what?"

They say you should never meet your heroes, that you will be disappointed. Not in this case. Meeting Dave was everything Andy hoped for and more, and for days afterwards he was buzzing.

"Pinch me," he said. "Did that really happen? Did we really sit on the side of the stage at a Foo Fighters' gig and hang out with Dave backstage after the show?"

Yes, it did and I will be forever grateful to the people that made it happen. Music was always such an important part of our lives and the psychological boost it gave Andy at that time was immeasurable.

With our wedding anniversary following six days after the gig, we felt like we had been given an early anniversary present. We were not big on celebrating wedding anniversaries.

"Every day should be a celebration of your marriage," my father had said, which sounds very deep and thoughtful but the reality was that Dad regularly failed to remember birthdays and anniversaries so it became his stock excuse.

This year, however, it was important. We wanted to spend a bit of time away together, celebrating our twenty-three years of married life, reflecting on what we had been through and how strong it had made us but also looking forward to more years to come.

We were hoping to fit in a trip to Amsterdam. There had been a time when Andy had travelled there almost every week for work and some of our closest friends, including Theo's godfather, lived in Holland. It helped that he was a renowned surgeon so if there was a problem with Andy we would have a medical contact nearby.

But Andy wasn't bouncing back from chemo like he used to and he was still struggling with the lingering fatigue from the radiotherapy. His bloods were showing that his liver function was not good so we decided that maybe it was best to minimise travelling and I found a lovely hotel in Bath for us to stay in. Even if Andy had to rest in the room for most of the day, at least he would be resting in luxury.

The day after the Foo Fighters' gig was a chemo bloods day. The routine was to go in to have bloods taken in the morning and then wait for the call to confirm that everything was okay for chemo to go ahead the following day. Since the SIRT treatment Andy had only managed a couple of rounds of reduced-strength chemo and we were waiting to see the outcome of the post-SIRT scans to work out what would happen next.

The pre-chemo bloods were not great, so the decision was made to delay chemo and try again in a few days but as the week progressed and our anniversary neared, Andy began feeling worse and worse. He was vomiting a lot and couldn't keep anything down. He was in pain and his stomach was swollen. I contacted the hospital ward.

"Bring him in straight away," was their response.

The atmosphere in the car was tense. Andy had clammed up and was irritated with my driving. He was irritated by everything and when I clipped the curb as I rounded a corner it was the final straw and he shouted at me.

"Stop fucking criticising me," I shouted back, all the worry spilling out. "I'm trying to help you and all you do is snap at me. Everyone else sees the happy Andy, why do you have to take all the anger and frustration out on me?"

"What if this is it, what if this is the beginning of the end?" he said, with tears in his eyes.

I was almost relieved by this outpouring of emotion. At last, he wasn't trying to put a positive spin on everything but was opening up about his feelings.

"Let's just get you to the hospital."

I felt instantly guilty for shouting. In that moment, so vulnerable and fed up with feeling ill, he was at the lowest point since his diagnosis. We had hit the wall.

When we got to the hospital the doctor ordered IV fluids to be put up straight away. Andy was very dehydrated.

"You are definitely staying in," said the ward sister as she took Andy's blood for testing.

His liver function numbers were very high. David, the oncologist, was worried. He sent Andy for an urgent scan. The SIRT had worked a little. The tumours had shrunk slightly but not enough to make things operable.

"We need to give the treatment a little more time to work. It's still early days," said David.

It would be a few weeks before we had the full picture of whether the tumours on his liver were operable so we held onto the fact that there had been a little bit of shrinkage. With time, maybe there would be enough to allow the one, small, awkwardly placed tumour to be moved away from the wall of the major blood vessel it was wrapped around.

But there was some bad news. Andy's liver was failing. It looked likely that he had developed a very rare reaction to the SIRT called radiation-induced liver damage. We had barely noted the very rare side effect possible with this treatment, even though it was documented in the literature. It was the first case that the oncologist had seen, but we do rare in our family.

There is a one in 1.25 million chance of giving birth to a child with Costello syndrome, and that's not factoring in all her other issues. Our child was a double jackpot odds gift so why shouldn't we have the same odds when it came to the rarest side effect of the radiotherapy treatment we'd felt so lucky Andy could have?

David took me to one side. He had been liaising with the specialist liver team in central London and Andy's liver numbers needed to start coming down otherwise he would have to be transferred to the intensive care unit for urgent treatment.

Andy had fluid in his abdomen and thick ankles from the water retention, signs that his liver was not working. He was jaundiced and his stomach was distended both by the fluid but also by his swollen liver. They started him on big doses of steroids and diuretics.

"Great," said Andy. "Even if I do manage to get any sleep with the steroids I'll be up all night peeing."

I was living off adrenaline as always, rushing between home and the hospital, trying to reassure the children, dropping medical supplies off at Daisy's hospice, where they had taken her in as an emergency case, and trying to support Andy.

The steroids had made him manic and he was buzzing, making plans for his return to work and developing new strategies for his business. I was pleased he had this distraction as I obsessively waited for the results of each blood test, hoping that his numbers had not climbed, and maybe even were starting to fall.

By our wedding anniversary there was a change. His liver was beginning to recover. He was out of danger. It was only then that he realised how sick he had been and how close to a one-way ticket to intensive care and life support.

We hugged each other tighter than ever as we shared a takeaway pizza and a cloudy lemonade on his hospital bed. No, it wasn't the luxury hotel I had imagined, but we were together, he had survived to tell the tale and fight another day. That was all that mattered.

CHAPTER TWENTY FOUR

"We are going to have to make some decisions about Daisy's surgery, we can't put it off any more."

With Andy reasonably stable and chemo stopped to allow his liver to fully recover from the radiation-induced liver damage, it was time to focus on Daisy.

Over the year we had been having conversations with her teams in Great Ormond Street about the pain she was experiencing, particularly with her bladder. Her mitrofanoff stoma, the channel that had been formed from her abdomen into her bladder using her appendix, was failing and it was causing huge pain every time we tried to insert a catheter to empty her bladder. She was on huge doses of painkillers and while we were managing to keep her reasonably stable, her quality of life was suffering.

It was not helped by her awareness that things were different at home and that Daddy was ill. She was having to spend more time being cared for by nurses at home or at respite while I cared for Andy, and this made it hard for her to deal with the pain, especially at night. All of this had a knock-on effect on her seizures, which were happening daily.

It was only when I was able to pause for breath from looking after Andy that I could see how much Daisy had deteriorated. She needed urgent surgery. But this surgery was going to be risky. Every time Daisy went to theatre for surgery it was risky. There were so many factors at play—her heart, her airway—that affected the success of the surgery. She had already come through so many big surgeries.

We had thought that those days were behind us but once again Andy and I were faced with the decision of whether or not we should sign the consent for Daisy to go to theatre to face an unknown outcome and an unknown length of recovery.

"We have to do it," we decided. We trusted her surgeon and everything he told us made sense. If the surgery worked it would improve her quality of life.

So, at the beginning of October, Daisy went to theatre. I lost count of the number of general anaesthetics she had been through in her short life. I think we were getting close to fifty plus. Certainly, the anaesthetists at Great Ormond Street knew her well and while she was classed as high risk, they had a protocol for managing her risks.

As we took her to theatre she held Andy's hand and signed 'home'.

"Very soon Daisy, very soon," he reassured her.

She loved her Daddy so much and smiled at him trustingly.

Eight hours we waited. Eight long, tense hours. Andy rested on the parents' bed in Daisy's room. It was a few weeks since he had been so ill and longer still since his last chemo and he was feeling better, certainly well enough to be with me at the hospital. I was glad and put the niggling worries I had about the delays in Andy's treatment and the obstacles we had encountered on the way to his own surgery to the back of my mind.

While we waited my imagination went into overdrive. What was happening in theatre? Was she going to be okay?

In my darkest moments, I thought that if she did die in surgery at least Andy and I could go through it together and she would not have to face the inevitable death of her darling Daddy at some point in her life. Selfishly I thought that I would have to bury two loved ones on my own if she outlived Andy. Fatigue and lack of food made my mind wander in all sorts of morbid directions.

Remarkably, Daisy came through and was stable. The surgery was incredible. Once they opened her up they found the adhesions and blockages in her bowel that were causing so much pain. Thirty centimetres of her small bowel was removed and used to enlarge her bladder, her stomas were moved and then came the big surprise: despite dozens of scans of her kidneys, no-one had yet picked up that she had two tubes coming out of one of her kidneys, a condition called duplex ureters. This possibly explained some of the infections she had been experiencing.

She had yet another big scar, tubes and drains coming out of her at strange angles, an epidural and morphine pump for the pain. All these things didn't shock us anymore. We knew exactly what each drip, drain and tube was for and when it would be removed.

And gradually they did come out and Daisy began her usual two steps forward, one step back road to recovery. The surgery had been a complete success, her mitrofanoff stoma now worked to empty her bladder and in combination with this newly enlarged bladder she had gained the biggest win—she no longer needed to wear nappies.

We thanked the surgeon for giving Daisy her dignity back.

She was acutely aware that she was a big girl and that nappies were for babies. At last she had a surgery that had given her something rather than just taken things away.

We could breathe a sigh of relief and plan for Daisy's recovery and eventual homecoming. There would be a couple more weeks in hospital, then a rehabilitation stay at the hospice to tweak her pain management regime.

I could relax a little and again focus on Andy. His final SIRT scan was due. This was the definitive one which would tell us if his liver was operable and all the stress and pain of the treatment had been worth it.

I caught the bus from Great Ormond Street across London to King's College Hospital, south of the river. Marion had brought Andy to his appointment and he was starving and therefore short-tempered. He hated having to be starved for scans, especially when on steroids.

Marion and I waited in the café while Andy had his scans. These ones would take longer than usual. The doctors needed to get the best picture possible to decide if there had been an improvement.

Then it was back to *scanxiety*. Andy and I tried to enjoy the time and put the worries about what the scan might show to the back of our minds. While Daisy recovered in hospital and the children were in school we fitted in some lunches in town. We loved to lunch and since being diagnosed with cancer, food had taken on an increasing importance in Andy's life.

Since his cancer diagnosis he had become obsessed with eating meat; his body was clearly crying out for the protein after twenty-two years of abstinence. Andy became a fully-fledged omnivore again and was keen to make up for lost time. Lunches tended to involve some restaurant or café he had seen reviewed in a magazine serving whatever his current craving was that day: Vietnamese, Turkish, Thai, Indian, Japanese. I didn't dare mention that I'd be happy with a cheese omelette.

Eventually Daisy transferred to Shooting Star-Chase for the next stage of her recovery. We were closer to home and as always it meant we could have precious family time together at the hospice knowing that Daisy was being well cared for.

Jules was struggling with anxiety so we decided to take him out of school for a few days. He had been so worried about Daisy while she was in hospital and he needed to spend some time near her to reassure himself that she was okay.

Andy was feeling strong again. His bloods were still not quite in the range where chemo was possible but at last he was able to get up and go for a walk and enjoy the day. He was also starting to plan his re-entry back into work.

His clients were desperately keen for him to come back, clamouring for his time. Equally, Andy was desperate to return to work now that he had less chemo fog. He was fed up with being a patient, fed up with talking about cancer. He wanted his old life back, to help others as he had always done, to earn money and feel valued.

He tentatively agreed to a phased programme of work with one of his clients to start in the new year, building in time for potential surgery and chemo and to allow him to recover between training and coaching sessions. He was so motivated and upbeat that I felt the old Andy was coming back to me. We were getting a bit of our life back. But the scans told a different story.

The SIRT had not done enough to shrink down the liver tumours to the point where they were operable. The primary tumour was also starting to grow a bit and a new metastasis had appeared in Andy's pelvis.

Despite everything, Andy's team remained upbeat. The plan was to allow his liver to fully recover from the damage it had sustained and then to restart chemo while some new radiology options were considered. We had to face the reality that maybe the liver would never be operable but with radiotherapy and chemotherapy the cancer could be kept in check. It wasn't great news but it wasn't all bad news.

"It could be worse," Andy remarked. "I'm still alive. There are still options, it's a crap hand but we'll work out the best way to play it. There is still plenty to play for."

CHAPTER TWENTY FIVE

"Happy Cancerversary to me!"

It was November, a year since Andy had been diagnosed with stage four metastasised colorectal cancer. It was a time for reflection. A year since Andy's diagnosis, seven years since Daisy had first started TPN.

Andy wrote on my blog:

Happy Cancerversary to me! So, if someone asked you what would you do if you had a year to live? What would you focus on, what would be important to you? What would you feel at the prospect of a limited life? As a family, we have lived with the knowledge of our own mortality since Daisy's birth and as a result we have always chosen to seize all the opportunities that come our way. We have had many talks about death and dying. This is the key to being happy, living without fear.

For me it has been straightforward to deal with things, my favourite phrase is, 'fuck it, what's the worst that can happen?'. If you already know the bottom line and are not afraid of it then fear has no power over you.

I choose to practice what I preach. I choose to be realistic and positive, it's served very well for the last year and will next too.

It has been a very tough transition for our children adjusting to our changed circumstances with everything else going on in their lives. They have done remarkably but we have always encouraged self-reliance and the attitude of 'if you want something you make it happen', don't accept excuses. Our role is to make them as independent as possible and able to make effective decisions for themselves. It's an attitude that has served Steph and I well over the years.

The sheer physical toll of the seventeen chemos (each a three-day infusion of some of the most potent chemicals known to science), the radiation, the drugs to manage the symptoms and the side effects have hit me hard, especially the last three months but I'm getting stronger day by day in small increments.

You learn to live with cancer fatigue. It's just so beyond tired and I have had to just adjust to what I can do rather than focus on what I am no longer able to do.

So, the cancer is incurable which is very different from terminal, by the way. I can live with it like many others who also live with an incurable cancer diagnosis and still have a great quality of life.

I have had such love from friends already close who have helped us practically or by just being there having a cup of tea and a chat. But also, I have caught up with people I haven't seen for years and made new friends over the course of the year. I'm so grateful for all the lunches, coffees, beer and most important sharing time with all of you. It gives me such energy and a boost.

There have been so many times over the last year where we have been laughing and weeping tears from the banter, silly pictures and piss taking, being told to check my 'cancer privilege' by my sixteen-year-old daughter Xanthe and my boys telling me to 'just get on with it, anyone would think you have something wrong with you!'

Humour, having fun and new experiences have been essential to feeling the way I am after a year and will continue to. Cancer has, of course, at the same time taken me to very dark places, in danger of not being able to recover, but I bounce back. Seeing the possibility of dying up close is such a huge thing to process, part of which is saying to yourself 'this is not the end, I will get better by facing it' and of course 'fuck it, what's the worst that can happen?'

I have experienced some of the worst pain in my life but it always fades as you cannot physically remember pain in the same way as experiences and emotions long past. This makes it easier sat in the toilet at 4am chanting 'all this will pass' along with the expletives that actually help to reduce pain.

The most emotional time is thinking about what I might miss out on in the future with my family and my soul mate. It's the thing that cuts the deepest and is the toughest thing to get my head around.

The cornerstone is of course Steph, I know you all should know by now what an amazing and incredible person she is and how much she achieves. From her running, her writing and then dealing with the daily phone calls from the multiple teams involved with Daisy's care as well as all the meetings and appointments to be scheduled for my care every week. She just makes it happen, no limiting beliefs.

On top of all of that she's helping me at every opportunity to make sure I keep taking the drugs, eating and hydrating. I would not be here if it wasn't for her.

So, we go again for another orbit around the sun and I can't wait for the next year as it will be different to this one with new experiences and some new opportunities seized. I mean this time last year I had no idea I would meet and hang out with Dave Grohl! Another great example of making something happen.

So, onward and upwards! Here we go again for another year and here's to being able to celebrate my second Cancerversary – 4th November 2016!

The chemo break initially helped Andy. He recovered from the radiation-induced liver disease and things were going in the right direction, but by mid-November there was a change.

We were out shopping in the bright, early winter sunlight and I noticed Andy's skin and eyes had a yellow pallor. I tried not to keep looking at him but over the days the jaundice became more obvious and it was soon followed by a pain in his right side.

We both made outwardly-positive noises but inside we were very worried. I became convinced that he had gallstones. Maybe the liver tumour had blocked his bile duct? That's okay, I thought, they can take out the bile duct, maybe debulk the tumour? I was becoming an amateur surgeon in my search for answers and solutions.

In hindsight you wonder why you can't see what is plainly happening in front of you but this is about life and death. In the moment, you cling to hope like the smallest piece of driftwood in an ocean of despair, and even if there is no way that piece of wood will get you back to land, you hope and plan. Maybe it will keep me going long enough for a passing ship to pick up us up.

The initial ultrasound did indeed show that Andy had gallstones. I knew from my research that this was not uncommon with cancer. I breathed a sigh of relief and tried to put Andy's increased yellow pallor and tiredness to the back of my mind.

David wanted him to have a more detailed CT scan of his liver to get a better picture of what was going on.

"Looks like you'll be getting surgery this side of Christmas after all," I said optimistically. "They will want to blast those gallstones to bring your bilirubin down."

It was not as simple as that. It never was but we were determined to be optimistic.

Andy's outpatient appointment was scheduled for the 25th November, the evening before his birthday. He was feeling good, even if he still looked a little yellow. He had been trying to walk every day to build up his strength and he certainly had his appetite back. We had booked a table at Nobu, probably the most expensive Japanese restaurant in London, for his birthday lunch.

We were waiting outside David's office. At last, he popped his head around the door and asked Diane, the oncology nurse, to come in as he was having problems with his computer. I suddenly had massive déjà vu back to that first-ever scan with Daisy when the obstetrician had left the room claiming computer problems. Something did not feel right.

As always, David was upbeat and considered. He had a habit of giving us the good news first to soften the blow. Andy's bloods were looking better, his liver function had improved a bit. He confirmed the scans had shown gallstones and there was some blockage of the bile duct as a result.

"The scans have also shown that the tumours have now infiltrated your liver," he said. "I think it's time to get community services involved as there is nothing more that can be done."

The room fell silent as we processed what he had just said.

"Is this it?" asked Andy.

"I'm afraid so," came the reply.

"I just didn't think it would be this quick." Tears rolled down Andy's cheeks. And then the next question. The one that he needed to ask but didn't want to know the answer to: *"How long?"*

"Weeks, possibly a couple of short months." I reached for Andy's hand. "It's his birthday tomorrow," I said.

CHAPTER TWENTY SIX

"I don't feel like I'm dying."

This was the end phase. This was the last of everything.

It was unbearable to think of telling the children. We needed time to let it sink in. This news was utterly unexpected.

"I don't feel like I'm dying," Andy said.

He had his sushi. We ordered the most expensive things on the menu—after all, we were never going to celebrate Andy's birthday at Nobu again.

We were never going to celebrate Andy's birthday again.

Later that day Andy broke the news to each of the older children individually. Each of them on their own, with their dad, as he told them that he had weeks to live. So brave, so sad. We didn't say anything to Daisy.

I asked around for advice. Where do you turn to find out how to tell a ten-year-old child with a learning disability that her daddy has weeks to live and very soon she will never ever see him again?

I contacted a friend who was living with untreatable cancer long term. She also had a child with a learning disability and had had more time to think about this sort of thing. She had been advised not to shield her child too much towards the end and to let them see the demise to a point.

Andy and I agreed that we would need to keep Daisy at home as much as possible so that she could see that Daddy was getting poorly and not getting better. We couldn't give her false hope and I would no longer be so positive about how Daddy was feeling when talking to her.

Andy needed to get to Scotland to see his family. Since his diagnosis he had reconnected with his Scottish roots; his parents had moved back to the Ayrshire coast soon after Theo was born and Andy had visited them a few times, catching up with extended family, visiting old childhood haunts, sharing stories.

No parent ever expects their child to die before them, no matter what their age. Andy's parents were devastated. Now he needed to go back there for the last time. To say his goodbyes.

We flew into Scotland on a cold, grey Saturday morning. It was trying to snow and Christmas shoppers were thronging the streets. We checked into a hotel in the centre of Glasgow, keen to enjoy time to ourselves before going to see Andy's parents.

While Andy slept, I walked around the city. We had been there earlier in the year, at Easter. The skies had been blue then, Andy had been able to walk and we were filled with such hope and optimism. It was such a contrast now, returning in winter.

The brashness of the Christmas lights seemed forced and wrong. I didn't even know if Andy was going to make it to Christmas. He wanted to. But Christmas was only a point in time: we needed to live in the here and now like never before.

We gathered in the bar that evening, a hastily convened

group of Andy's brother and nephew, his old school friend and my old school friend. If anyone had seen us they would never have guessed that we were there to toast a dying man. We drank and laughed, cried a little, shared raucous stories and left the bar feeling enveloped in love and happiness. It was a wonderful evening, a time to say all that needed to be said, a time to celebrate. A time to live.

We got to Andy's parents' house the next day. As always with Scottish families there was food, lots of it. You must never leave the house hungry.

"Would you like a cup of tea, son?" his mum asked, not quite sure what to do or say, but Andy was not one to dim the lights and sit solemnly.

"Let's crack open the Champagne," he declared.

And that set the tone for the afternoon. His aunts, uncles and cousins came to visit and they all pored over old photo albums and shared stories. We drank champagne and sang *'Happy Birthday'* to Andy.

The toughest part was when it came to say goodbye, to walk out of the door knowing that he was going home to die, that he would never see his parents or his brother again. That the next time they came to our home would be for his funeral. We hugged and cried on the doorstep and I watched Andy embrace his parents.

We sat in silence on the plane, letting the enormity of it all wash over us. When we arrived home, I wrote a blog post to tell our friends around the world what was happening. Many of them had shared our journey with Daisy from the early days.

30th November 2015, St Andrew's Day.
Andy was born on the 26th of November in Kilmarnock,

Scotland. His parents registered his birth on St Andrew's Day, giving him the name Andrew Paul in honour of the Scottish patron saint. So we thought St Andrew's Day would be a good day to tell you some sad news.

Last week Andy was told that the cancer his medical team had worked so hard to make operable was now infiltrating the liver and no further active treatment options were available.

His care is now palliative, supporting his symptoms in order to make him as comfortable as possible during this final phase.

We always knew this time would come; we just did not expect it to come so soon—a year, five years—the outcome was always going to be the same. The brilliant medical care Andy has had has given us a year. And what a year.

When you know your time is limited you have to seize every moment. We learned this early on with Daisy. We knew that our time together as a family of six would be shorter than most; we just did not think that it would be Andy who would go first. But as we always say, it is what it is and while it is so sad, Andy's diagnosis has created the most precious opportunity to say goodbye and plan for a good death.

We are enjoying this time together, seeing friends, fitting in a twenty-four-hour visit to family in Scotland, looking at old photos, sharing memories and having the biggest laughs as we remember all the incredible things we have done and the people who have been part of Andy's journey. We feel privileged to have this time to prepare and say goodbye.

Seize the moment and take nothing for granted.

The outpouring of love was palpable and it gave Andy such comfort to know how much he was loved and the impact he had made on so many lives over the years. Friends called and wrote and many of our closest friends made huge efforts to come and visit Andy, just to spend time with him, share some moments with him, tell him how much they loved him.

I had to balance the outpouring of love with Andy's need for rest and the need for our children to spend time with him, as well as my own need to spend time together with my husband.

I was still running around managing Daisy's care during those times without a nurse. Andy was still trying to get out and about, walking around the block, getting some fresh air, staying as active as he could.

"I really don't feel like I'm dying," he would remark and I would rub his back and say, "I know, Andy," wondering what it all meant.

But he was getting more fatigued, and the jaundice and fluid retention were beginning to take their toll.

We met with the palliative consultant to discuss end-of-life plans. This was incredibly important for both of us. I needed to know Andy's wishes so that I could support them at the end. He needed to know what would happen. What is it like to die from end-stage liver failure caused by colorectal cancer?

"You will start to lose your appetite," the consultant explained. "And you will become more and more fatigued. You will sleep more and more. We will give you some morphine through a syringe driver and we will also give you some midazolam as you may start to become confused and that may distress you. We will aim to keep you as pain-free as possible. We will be able to top up the morphine and manage your symptoms. Eventually you will sleep all the time and then you will fall unconscious."

Andy decided that he wanted to die at home and he was assured that he could change his mind at any point. He made it clear that he did not want to be resuscitated or to have a prolonged medicalised death. He just wanted to be pain-free and at home.

We both felt good to have had the conversation with the palliative consultant. Daisy had been cared for by a paediatric palliative consultant for a few years and the term did not scare us.

Andy had accepted his fate from day one; the clock was ticking; his cancer was incurable and he was going to die. He felt cheated of the extra time he had hoped his treatment was going to buy him but I could sense his resignation; it was not a battle he could win.

We sat down together a couple of days later and planned his funeral. Living with Daisy meant that we were very comfortable with talking about death. We had lived in anticipation of her death for over a decade. We had not realised that she would outlive one of her parents.

Andy was insistent that his funeral had to be a celebration with music, friends and a party afterwards.

"What about the dress code?" I asked. "People will want to know, should they wear black?"

He thought for a while then said, "Tell people to make an effort."

So typical of Andy. He'd have people turning up in ball gowns and dinner suits if he could.

We discussed the songs he wanted played. He wanted to be cremated, and we talked about where I would take his ashes afterwards. These were not sad conversations—they were very typical of us, Andy and Steph. They were practical conversations, with laughter and jokes and moments of overwhelming sadness. We focused on the details because they helped us deal with the reality.

Our time together was racing by: Christmas was on the horizon, Daisy's birthday just before. I was trying to plan for these two events not knowing if Andy would be around to enjoy them but wanting to keep some normality for the rest of the family.

And finally, Andy was able to complete the second item on his bucket list. He had wanted to see Arsenal win the FA Cup final. Technically he had, but he was sat at home in front of the TV watching it while his chemo ran. Arsenal were storming to the top of the Premiership and some kind friends organised for us all to go to the next home match as guests of the club.

We walked out to the pitch before the teams arrived and Andy's back visibly straightened as he breathed in the atmosphere, soaked up the energy. He loved that place, that football club, and was so happy to have one last chance to see the team play.

Not only did Arsenal win that day but Andy bumped into three of his former work colleagues in the bar. We got home and after I put Daisy to bed and set up her intravenous drugs for the evening, I joined Andy on the sofa to watch '*Match of the Day*' and promptly fell asleep. He was wide awake, commenting on Facebook, texting friends. Contented, happy. He had seen Arsenal win today; he had met Dave Grohl and watched the Foo Fighters play a few weeks previously. He was sat on the sofa with the wife he loved, his children asleep upstairs. Life was good.

CHAPTER TWENTY SEVEN

"I'm tired Steph, I don't think I'm going to make it downstairs today."

Not surprisingly Andy was exhausted the next day. He could not get out of bed. Friends had driven over from Holland and Belgium and they took turns to come upstairs and spend time with him.

The physical tiredness was secondary to the emotional exhaustion. Seeing other people's sadness and grief as they struggled to come to terms with having to say goodbye was taking its toll.

The next day Andy could not stop vomiting. He was becoming uncomfortable and was clearly dehydrated.

"I know you don't want to, but I am going to have to take you to the ward to be assessed. You probably need some IV fluids," I insisted.

My years of training with Daisy, understanding fluid balances and reading the signs, had served me well.

I was reaching capacity with my caring roles. I had to get Andy to hospital while bringing Daisy along as we had no nursing cover. I left him there while I rushed to drop her off at respite. Our other children were off school. We wanted as much time together as a family as possible, and the older three could be left at home while I was running around.

IV fluids perked him up and when I got back Andy was consulting the menu and deciding whether he should have some hummus, bread and olives or choose something more substantial. He also had some news for me.

"They might be able to do a palliative procedure on my liver which could buy me some more time," he said.

Andy's gastroenterologist, the one who had first found the cancer, paid him a visit. He'd had some success with a new procedure which involved drilling microscopic holes into the liver to try and relieve some of the pressure caused by the tumours. There were no guarantees it would work, but it could potentially buy Andy some precious time. We had a little glimmer of hope, and we certainly needed it. Andy was deteriorating rapidly.

Friends continued to visit and keep Andy company whenever I could not be there with him. And then a crisis hit, one that I had been dreading.

Daisy became ill at the same time that Andy was in hospital. She was having cluster seizures, one after the other, tonic-clonic seizures with minimal breaks in between. She was not responding to the midazolam rescue medication and needed to be blue-lighted to A&E.

I was torn. I needed to be with Andy who was becoming sicker and sicker by the day but I also needed to be with Daisy who was in an acute crisis which could easily go either way. I didn't dare think about my other three children back home, holding the fort, being brave, carrying on as normal.

We tried Daisy's second line of rescue medication, another big infusion of sedative, but she kept convulsing.

"Not today, not today," I pleaded with her. The thought of losing two of them in a matter of weeks was unbearable.

We tried a third line medication while the consultant started to make noises about intubation and intensive care transfers. Thankfully it worked. Daisy sank into an exhausted sleep and I left her in the care of the nurses while I rushed back to Andy in the specialist cancer hospital overlooking Wimbledon Common.

As I was driving back my mobile rang. It was David, the oncologist.

"I'm concerned about this palliative procedure that is being proposed," he said. "I think it may be just too risky. I think Andy is too sick to survive it."

"You want me to speak to him, don't you?" I said.

"I don't think he really understands the risks," continued David.

I decided to wait until the next day to have that conversation. Andy was tired and I just wanted to sit with him, to be in his presence, enjoy the peace and our time alone.

"We talked about making sure you don't have a medicalised death," I reasoned with him the next day. "You need to think long and hard about the implications of going for this procedure—what happens if things don't go to plan."

I left it there. It had to be Andy's decision but I could see that he was not strong enough for a general anaesthetic. I didn't even know if tomorrow he would be strong enough for a hospital transfer as the procedure could not be done locally. Just getting out of bed to sit in a chair was a huge effort and his mind was beginning to lose focus. It was the beginning of the end.

"Take me home, Steph," he said to me the next day when he eventually woke. He was in need of more and more pain and anti-sickness medication and was vomiting constantly as his swollen liver pushed on his stomach.

We had nurse cover at home and my mum had come to stay to look after Theo, Xanthe and Jules and help keep the house running so that I could focus on Andy.

It takes a long time to leave hospital when you have had a baby. You can't just go. Forms need to be filled in, community services informed. It was the same with bringing Andy home to die. It was a cold and wet Friday afternoon. Not the best day to get community nursing services in place. A referral had been made to the local hospice for palliative nursing outreach but all of this can take some time to set up.

We borrowed a wheelchair from the ward and eventually, after a long, frustrating afternoon of telephone calls and form filling, I wheeled Andy out of the ward and the hospital for the very last time.

When we got home our log burner was blazing and his chair was next to it in the sitting room.

"I've got the TV all ready for you Dad," Theo was waiting for him.

I didn't like to point out that setting it up to show the latest episode of '*The Walking Dead*' was maybe not the right thing to be watching right now.

Andy had a few sips of his favourite beer from the brewery in Suffolk that we had visited only a few months previously. I wheeled him around the ground floor of the house, showing him the gloriously framed print of a David Bowie portrait we had bought a couple of years previously at the Victoria & Albert Museum. It had languished behind our sofa for ages until I decided it had to be framed so Andy could see it on the wall and know that it was there.

He was exhausted and wanted to go to bed. Daisy was already upstairs, the nurse preparing her TPN drip and meds. I was grateful we had fought so hard for the home adaptations that had meant Daisy's room was upstairs, accessible by a stair-lift. Andy could now use that lift to get to our bedroom and lie down in his own bed.

He slowly inched his way into the bedroom, every step a huge effort, flinching with pain, exhausted from the journey home. He lay down in bed and relaxed. Even the duvet was too heavy and painful to bear. I fetched a fleece blanket from Daisy's room. He drifted off into a fitful sleep and I began to unpack his meds and put the contact details for the on-call nurses into my phone.

I went into Daisy's room and began to draw up Andy's IV meds. Nothing could have prepared me for that moment when, having learned how to prepare my own daughter's IV medication, I would find myself doing the same thing for her daddy. They both had the same anti-sickness meds.

Theo brought in the guest bed that we kept in his room and I made it up for the night. I was not going to leave Andy's side.

Daisy knew Daddy was home. I firmly believe she knew in her own way that he was home to die. I told her the next day that Daddy was in bed with a very poorly tummy. I avoided using positives as I had been advised, just keeping it factual and telling her Mummy and the nurses were looking after Daddy.

Our other children accepted it too. They had known that this time would come. They were happy that Andy was back home and that we could be a family, that they could come and go and spend time with him.

Jules especially enjoyed sitting with Andy and talking to him when he was awake. Theo was very practical. Xanthe, always the strong, brave one, was scared and overwhelmed. She was afraid to show her emotions. I was worried about her and when Marion came over to see Andy, I asked her if she could take Xan out for a walk and a chat. It helped her to open up to someone else. She was so used to having to be practical and hold things together and she was only sixteen.

The palliative care nurses came the next day and set up a syringe driver with a continuous drip of morphine and midazolam. This helped Andy relax and it also made him more sleepy. He was talking less and less and spending more time sleeping. I lay next to him the next night with my hand on his chest.

"I'm with you, I'm not leaving you," I whispered to him, afraid to close my eyes despite being exhausted.

I had stopped all visitors now, except for Marion and Simon, who was Andy's closest friend and my sister's ex-husband. It was his wish that they were the last visitors he saw.

"I don't understand it," I said to Marion when I came downstairs to eat some food and see the children. "He's hanging on when he said he didn't want to linger."

"Have you given him permission?" she replied. "Maybe he's waiting for you to tell him it's okay to leave."

I told him. But still he kept breathing, strong, determined breaths, with moments of lucidity when he would speak a brief couple of words to the children or give a thumbs up to their questions. The children drifted in and out of the room, playing on their video games when not with him, updating their friends online, waiting for the inevitable.

Daisy was still in the house and this was worrying me. I was aware that in the next room, while I lay next to Andy and his nurses came and went, Daisy was next door, with her nurse.

Her incredible hospice organised for Daisy to be transferred there as an emergency admission the next day. At least I would know she would be happy and distracted and I could focus 100 percent on Andy.

One of Andy's nurses sat with him while I ran around packing Daisy's things for her stay at Shooting Star Chase. Her taxi had arrived and her homecare nurse helped her out of bed to her lift. Suddenly I knew what I needed to do.

I threw open our bedroom door and said to Daisy, "Say 'bye-bye' to Daddy!"

"Bye, Daddy," she shouted, waving at the doorway as her stair-lift moved downwards.

Andy had been semi-conscious all morning but he summoned every last bit of strength he had in his body, raised his hand and said, "Bye".

I knew then why he was waiting. He needed to know that his little girl was in a safe place and would not be there when he died. We had given the older children the option to choose what they wanted to do but he knew that this was not an option we could give Daisy. Andy had chosen to wait until she had left.

Within thirty minutes of Daisy's leaving, Andy's breathing had changed, his eyes closed and his body began to close down. I held his hand until my rock, my soulmate, the love of my life, took his last breath and was gone.

CHAPTER TWENTY EIGHT

"He's gone."

14th December 2015

In the end the children decided not to be in the room when Andy died. As always, each of them dealt with it in their own individual way. Theo's girlfriend came over and they went out to meet up with his friends, Xanthe retreated to her room to her laptop and her friends, Jules wanted to be with me. He came into the room to see Andy and stroked his hair.

"He was the best dad in the world," he said through the tears.

He was. He was a brilliant dad. Even at the very end of his life he was thinking about his children.

But now I had to start making the inevitable phone calls, to tell his parents, his brother, his cousins, that he had gone. It was draining and it still hadn't sunk in.

The community nurses came to remove the syringe driver, wash him and lay him out ready for the undertakers. I took his wedding ring off and put it on my finger. I sprayed his favourite cologne on him. He would have liked that.

I couldn't face telling Daisy yet. Everything was all too

soon. I needed time to process it myself. I sat and listened to the radio, drinking wine. Jo Whiley played '*Everlong*' by the Foo Fighters as her last song. The tears poured down my face.

The undertakers had been to the house earlier that afternoon and when I got into bed there was still a dent where Andy had lain. It felt comforting to lie there, on his side of the bed. I fell into a fitful, exhausted, wine-fuelled sleep.

The next morning my mobile pinged with a text.

Get t'kettle on.

It was Andy's brother, John. He had driven through the night from Scotland and had slept in his car outside. Andy would have been overwhelmed with gratitude and love. John had booked into a hotel a couple of miles away so he could be around but not breathing down our necks. It was just what I, and the children, needed.

There was another text. It was my friend Ali. She was on her way to be with me, just has she had been the day I met Andy.

Ali, John and I drove to the hospice to see Daisy. I went into her room and shut the door. She knew what was coming; she understood so much more than her communication skills allowed her to tell us. I climbed into bed and cuddled her.

"You know Daddy had a very poorly tummy, don't you?" She stopped playing with her iPad and put it down. "Well, sadly, the doctors couldn't fix it because it was a special poorly."

She drew the side of her hand vertically down her face. The Makaton sign for '*sad*'.

"Daddy died—that means we won't be able to see him anymore. But we will always be able to talk about him, and think about him and remember all the lovely things we all did together."

We looked at photos and talked about Andy.

"Daddy loved you very much, you know that don't you, Daisy?"

Daisy crossed her arms across her chest, the Makaton sign for 'love'.

"Love Daddy," she said. "Bye-bye Daddy."

It was the hardest thing I have ever had to do.

Daisy was one week away from her eleventh birthday, just after that it was Christmas and I had now broken the news that no little girl should ever have to hear. I wanted to curl up and hide under a duvet but we had Daisy's birthday and Christmas to get through and on top of this there was a funeral to organise.

Great timing, Andy, I thought wryly, knowing full well that he had so wanted to try and hang on until the new year so that Christmas would not be ruined for the children.

Thankfully, as always, Daisy's hospice saved the day. They took care of Daisy's birthday, organising a party and presents for her.

I asked the children what they wanted to do for Christmas. The offer was on the table for all of us to stay at the hospice and I secretly hoped they would agree as it would mean I could hand over Daisy's medical care to the nurses. But all of them wanted to be home, in our own house, where so many memories had been made. They needed to be home.

On Christmas Eve, I put their presents under the tree and hung stockings on each of the bedroom doors just as Andy and I had done every year since Theo's birth. This was it. I was flying solo. Now it was down to me to mark these occasions, make memories with our children. To be there at all these important moments, the good ones and the bad ones.

New Year's Eve was harder still. I did not want 2015 to end.

2015 was the year Andy had died and left us, but with every minute that passed we were closer to it becoming *last* year. I was leaving Andy behind. It was too soon.

We hadn't had the funeral, yet Christmas had come and gone and we were already saying goodbye to 2015. It was so unfair. I wanted time to stand still. Just give me a chance to say my own goodbyes.

So many people wanted to say goodbye to Andy that I decided to hold a memorial and a funeral service. I didn't want our friends and family to have to go back to work and school knowing that this was still hanging over them. It had also been a nightmare booking a crematorium for the weekend after New Year's Eve but in the end we had a plan and the perfect way for everyone to say their goodbyes to Andy.

On 2nd January 2016, 200 friends and family gathered in the gothic hall of Andy's old drama school in London. Christmas lights were still hung at the windows and the Christmas trees were shedding pine needles in anticipation of the Twelfth Night.

We held a beautiful celebration of Andy's life with words and music from friends from all walks of his life, work colleagues, acting friends, family. In between the moving tributes we played music chosen by Andy.

Afterwards we moved to the bar to hold the party that Andy was so adamant should take place. Here, new friendships were forged, stories were told, glasses were raised. Oh, he would have loved it. People had flown in from all over the world and had, as he had requested, 'made an effort'. Many friends wore Arsenal shirts in his honour. The outpouring of love for my husband was palpable. His legacy existed in the impact he'd had on so many lives in the room that evening.

Thirty-six hours later the hearse arrived at our house with

the wicker coffin and simple arrangement of thistles along with white roses like the ones from our wedding. This was when it all hit. Saturday night was Andy's party. Today was the last goodbye. The mood was sombre; this was going to be tough.

Daisy would not be coming. It would be too confusing for her so she was away in respite for a couple of days. We planned to release some balloons with her later that month so she could say her own goodbye to Daddy.

Theo, Xanthe and Jules were so brave. All eyes would be on them today.

Clearly Andy felt we should all lighten up. I had decided that we should travel to the crematorium in our campervan, following the hearse, with family and friends behind us. Keith was driving the van and had taken it to the garage that morning to fill up with fuel for the short journey to the crematorium. We pulled away to follow the hearse and the van stalled. Keith restarted it.

"It's just been serviced and has been running fine," I said. "The engine's probably cold or something."

Then it stalled again.

I turned to Keith. "You did put petrol in when you filled it up didn't you?"

"Er, nope," he replied as the realisation dawned. "Diesel."

So, the mood turned from sombre and dark to farcical as I jumped out of the van to flag down the hearse and everyone got out of their cars to push the van back onto the drive.

"He's having the last laugh, Keith," I said as we set off again in our other car.

"Bloody Nimrod," he replied. "He'll haunt me forever now for killing his beloved van!"

I walked behind the hearse as we arrived at the crematorium.

A piper walked in front, playing a lament. The sun was shining. We were making our last journey together, just Andy and me. I needed to have this last special moment with him.

The piper finished playing and Andy's friends brought him into the chapel while *'London Calling'* by The Clash played out over the PA. The children and I laid his football scarves over the coffin and put the hat Andy always wore to festivals on top of it. We lit four candles, one for each of the beautiful lights he had brought into the world: Theo, Xanthe, Jules and Daisy.

Theo stood up to speak. He looked around the packed chapel, shrugged his shoulders and began his tribute.

"It's a bit shit, isn't it?" he started.

That summed it up.

There were tears, laughter and music, beautiful tributes and then it was time to say goodbye, the lyrics of Bowie's *'Starman'* taking on extraordinary significance as we filed out into the sharp, wintry air.

That night, I sat alone in the garden and gazed up at the clear sky. Andy always said that when we die our energy just transfers on. Perhaps a few atoms that were Andy were now there dancing among the stars.

I raised my glass to him.

"Good night starman, it was one hell of a ride."

EPILOGUE

I sit here now, trying to adjust to the new phase in my life. There was before Andy, with Andy, with children, with Daisy and now there is without Andy.

I went back to Atlantic College. It was thirty years since we all left, full of hope that we would change the world: young, wide-eyed works-in-progress, enthusiastic, naive. Now I am learning to walk a new path. I am a widow, a mother of four children who still need me.

When a person loses a limb, they still feel phantom pain. This is what it's like when you lose the person who has been your life. Someone told me that when you have a soulmate, your DNA becomes melded with theirs and you become one. A part of me has gone and now I am learning to walk again.

You can't sugarcoat my story. I see people recoil in shock when I tell them. I have built up a wall of resilience.

"Oh, it's okay, I'm managing, it is what it is," I say to the shocked faces.

People can't bear to imagine what it must feel like to be me, to suffer this sort of loss. And yet I don't want this to be my identity. Widow, carer, mother, somewhere in all of this there is still that girl who left school thirty years ago, full of hopes and dreams. I still have hopes and dreams. I still have a life. I am thriving, I am not just surviving.

It was Andy who taught me how.

POSTSCRIPT

Today our beautiful, feisty, determined girl, Daisy Rose, took her last breath and is out of pain and dancing in the stars with her beloved daddy.

At 2.45pm her life support was switched off and Theo and I held her hands as she passed away. Jules, Xanthe, Theo and I surrounded her with love as she left us to go to a place where she can run and jump and skip and play to her heart's content and be Daisy, not a syndrome, a diagnosis, just a little girl.

I have a certificate that says she died of septic shock but I think it was just her time to go. Her little body was slowing down, she was needing more and more medications and painful procedures and over the past few weeks she just preferred to lie in bed and let us come to her. She missed her daddy so much and talked about him every single day. I think her heart broke when he left us.

We were honoured to have her in our lives for twelve years. Twelve years where she not only defied the odds but truly lived.

No one who met Daisy ever forgot her; she changed so many lives, left such a beautiful legacy. She gave me purpose, meaning and direction—along with a few more grey hairs than I should have at this age—but my life and the life of her brothers and sister have been made so much more meaningful by her presence.

Daisy deteriorated very quickly and she just wanted to go home. It was not possible but thanks to our hospice and the cold mattress they set up in her room we brought her home this evening for one last night in her own bed, surrounded by her toys. She looks like she is fast asleep and any minute will wake up and tell us, as only Daisy could, to 'go'. Tomorrow we will take her to her beloved Shooting Star Chase Hospice, just as we always planned.

Theo thanked the ICU consultant for allowing her a dignified death. We will always be grateful to Great Ormond Street Hospital for being there for Daisy on her final journey and for never, ever giving up on her.

I cannot believe that she has gone. She defied the odds over and over and was determined to make her mark on the world. She did.

Daisy Rose Nimmo
Sunrise—22nd December 2004
Sunset—31st January 2017

About the Author

Stephanie Nimmo is a London-based writer, mother, music-lover, carer, widow, bereaved parent, runner and all-round plate spinner. She's still trying to have a life, despite life's unexpected twists and turns. Stephanie started writing about her life (caring for her youngest daughter who had a rare genetic condition) as a way of documenting what was happening, but also in order to share an insight into a world and a life that she previously knew nothing about. The blog grew and grew in popularity and is now read by tens of thousands of people around the world.

As her family's life became increasingly complicated Stephanie's blog was not only therapeutic, but it also helped educate a wider audience on the realities of caring not only for a complex child but a terminally ill husband. Stephanie Nimmo's experiences have shown her to possess an incredible resilience she never knew she had, it has shaped her and she believes that we are all shaped by what happens to us.

"We can't choose our life's path, much as we try, the unexpected will always happen, but it's how we respond to it that makes the difference. I decided to write my book after my husband passed away as I not only wanted to share our story but also share that we should take nothing for granted in life. I really have had to seize the day and I hope that my book will inspire readers to reflect on their own lives and how they choose to respond to what happens to them."

Find out more at www.stephnimmo.com
Twitter: @stephnimmo
Instagram: @stephnimmo
Facebook.com/wasthisintheplan
Blog: www.wasthisintheplan.co.uk